CONTENTS

HOW TO BECOME A CHRISTIAN

LIFE BY DESIGN

We live in a broken world. This brokenness is seen in suffering, violence, poverty, pain, and death around us. Brokenness leads us to search for a way to make life work.

The Bible tells us that God originally planned a world that worked perfectly—where everything and everyone fit together in harmony. God made each of us with a purpose—to worship Him and walk with Him (Gen. 1:31 and Ps. 19:1).

Life doesn't work when we ignore God and His original design for our lives. We selfishly insist on doing things our own way. The Bible calls this sin. Sin leads to a place of brokenness. The consequence of our sin is separation from God—in this life and for all of eternity (Rom. 3:23 and Rom. 6:23).

We need a remedy—some good news. Because of His love, God did not leave us in our brokenness. Jesus, God in human flesh, came to us and lived perfectly according to God's design. Jesus came to rescue us—to do for us what we could not do for ourselves. He took our sin and shame to the cross, paying the penalty of our sin by His death. Jesus was then raised from the dead—to provide the only way for us to be rescued and restored to a relationship with God (John 3:16; Col. 2:14; and 1 Cor. 15:3-4).

We cannot escape this brokenness on our own. We need to be rescued. We must ask God to forgive us—turning from sin to trust in Jesus. This is what it means to repent and believe. Believing, we receive new life through Jesus. God turns our lives in a new direction (Mark 1:15; Eph. 2:8-9; and Rom. 10:9).

When God restores our relationship to Him, we begin to discover meaning and purpose in a broken world. Now we can pursue God's design in all areas of our lives. God's Spirit empowers us to recover His design and assures us of His presence in this life and for all of eternity (Phil. 2:13 and Eph. 2:10).

Now that you have heard this good news, God wants you to respond to Him. You can talk to Him using words like these: My life is broken—I recognize it's because of my sin. I believe Christ came to live, die, and was raised from the dead—to rescue me from my sin. Forgive me. I turn from my selfish ways and put my trust in You. I know that Jesus is Lord of all, and I will follow Him.

MEET THE WRITERS

KIMA JUDE wrote the teaching plans for this resource. She is a member of The Oaks Baptist Church in Grand Prairie, Texas, where she leads the women's ministry and her husband Barry serves as pastor. Kima has a bachelor's degree in journalism from Marshall University and had an early career as a newspaper reporter followed by a freelance writing career. She has written for several Christian publications, including Lifeway's *January Bible Study* and several *Explore the Bible* group plans.

She is employed full-time at a local university in the Dallas-Fort Worth region directing foundation relations and writing proposals. She and her husband are the parents of four young adult children and three young grandchildren. She looks forward to helping them discover the wonders of the Bible.

ARGILE SMITH wrote the expositor's notes for this resource. Argile serves as pastor of Parkway Baptist Church, Biloxi, Mississippi. He's a graduate of William Carey College (BA) and New Orleans Baptist Theological Seminary (MDiv, PhD).

© 2023 Lifeway Press® • Printed in the United States of America • ISBN: 978-1-0877-8368-0 • Item: 005842157

Subject Area: Bible Studies, Dewey Decimal Classification Number: 226.9
Subject Heading: Bible Gospels and Acts—Sermon on the Mount—Study and Teaching/ Christian Life
Lifeway Christian Resources • 200 Powell Place, Suite 100 • Brentwood, TN 37027-7707

TEACHING PLANS

YOUR NOTES

JESUS'S (SHOCKING) VISION FOR THE TRULY BLESSED LIFE

Before the Session:

a. Review Matthew 5:1-16 from the Bible, highlighting repeated words, ideas that stand out to you, and Jesus's directives that seem especially countercultural.

b. Read the Sermon on the Mount Introduction and chapter 1 in the Personal Study Guide as well as the related Expository Notes in this Leader Guide.

c. Pray for the group who will be engaged in the January Bible Study.

d. Gather Personal Study Guides, extra Bibles, and pens for the group.

e. Be prepared to display **Teaching Item 1: Happiness word**; **Teaching Item 2: Flourish word**; **Teaching Item 3: Thrive word**, and **Teaching Item 4: Blessed word** by downloading and printing or projecting.

f. Be prepared to display **Teaching Item 5: Sermon on the Mount Illustration**.

g. Practice reading the sermon aloud as you imagine Jesus would have delivered it.

Leading the Session:

1. Introduce the session by drawing attention to **Teaching Item 1: Happiness word** and invite the group to share definitions of the word. Add **Teaching Item 2: Flourish word** and invite the group to share their definition of this word. Draw attention to **Teaching Item 3: Thrive word** and invite the group to share a definition. Encourage the group to decide whether any of these words have been goals in their lives.

Introduce the study of the Sermon of the Mount by noting that the words recorded in Matthew were spoken directly by Jesus to an audience of disciples and seekers. Set the stage for studying this famous sermon by helping your group of listeners imagine the scene: Jesus, on a mountain, delivering a message while sitting down, surrounded by a throng of people hanging on every word. Display **Teaching Item 5: Sermon on the Mount Location**.

Call on a volunteer to read the opening to the Sermon on the Mount, Matthew 5:1-2. Invite the group to review the Introduction to determine the significance of 1) being on a mountaintop and 2) sitting down. Briefly discuss how they may picture this scenario, such as in an amphitheater-type setting. Direct the group to complete **Friends in High Places** activity in page 16 of the PSG for more insight on the mountain setting.

Direct the group's attention to the entire passage to be studied during the session and tell them that you are going to attempt to share it the way you thought Jesus may

YOUR NOTES

have delivered His message. Note that you could have the wrong artistic interpretation—perhaps He was more fiery or more restrained and undoubtedly more compelling. Move your chair to a place where most of the group can see you—even if it's in the middle of the room—and read Matthew 5:1-16 aloud. Draw attention back to the words that the group has defined: *happiness, flourish, thrive*. Note that none of these words are found in the passage translation—instead another word, which may be considered a synonym or related, is: *blessed*. Display **Teaching Item 4: Blessed word** and encourage the group to consider how they would define it. Draw attention to the PSG, page 12 where the writer points out that there are actually two definitions for the word *blessed*, one an act of distributing divine favor and the other a state of being. Emphasize that while we tend to think of sermons as a set of instructions, often negative, that the writer makes the point that Jesus is not issuing commands in His message but describing a state of mind that these actions produce in a Christian. Invite the group to think of other words that may characterize this and be prepared to suggest a few more: *peace, serenity, satisfaction, contentment, bliss*, and so forth. Draw attention back to the word strips to ask: **Would you say that you live in a state of happiness? Are you flourishing? Are you thriving? Are you blessed?** Note that in some ways this part of the Sermon on the Mount is a good test of understanding how close we are to kingdom life.

Guide the group to search the PSG, page 17 to learn why. Point out that while *beatus* is a Greek word, it makes perfect sense in English to also think of the Beatitudes as Be Attitudes, or ways to live a whole and flourishing life. Note that there are eight Beatitudes outlined in the passage, all of which work together to provide a comprehensive picture of a flourishing follower of Jesus Christ.

Invite a volunteer to take your seat and read Matthew 5:3-6, challenging that person to share it in a way they imagine Jesus may have. Guide the group to underline all the words that indicate who is blessed: the poor, mourning, humble, hungry, and thirsty. Ask: **Are these attributes that you would normally assign to "blessed" people?**

Encourage the group to break down each phrase for meaning and application. Challenge the group to discuss diverse ways we can be impoverished, beyond the scarcity of earthly goods. Define grief as mourning that may go beyond personal loss. Talk about what humility looks like in our contemporary culture. Point to ways that we hunger and thirst for righteousness that extends to others. Direct the group to the PSG, page 19, to complete the **Be Attitudes** exercise.

Ask the group to share their definition of the word *paradox* and inquire whether Jesus outlined a series of paradoxes in this passage. Point out that poverty, humility, hunger, and thirst all have significant spiritual context yet none are left in a state of want. Highlight that the counter point to each Beatitude seems to nullify any negativity that may be associated with poverty, grief, humility, hunger, and thirst. Invite the group to share testimonies of their own experiences with such paradoxes.

2. Call on a second volunteer to read the next set of Beatitudes from Matthew 5:7-9. Guide the group to highlight the words that describe happy disciples in this passage. Note the shift from the first set of Beatitudes, which were focused on God, to a focus on others and draw a parallel to the

YOUR NOTES

first and second commandments. Inquire: **What's your emotional reaction to this set of words? If you find them inherently more appealing, why? Do you admire these attributes when you see them in others?** Take a few minutes to define each term: *mercy* as compassion, *purity* as a life of integrity, and *peacemaking* as pursuing reconciliation.

Discuss the circular nature of this set of Beatitudes, noting that the Bible consistently teaches that the attitudes that we exhibit come back to us through others. Discuss the Golden Rule and its promise, noting that you will delve into that deeper in a later session. Also discuss the admonition not to judge to avoid being judged. Talk about whether mercy, purity, or peacemaking, while always desirable, may be challenging. Remind the group that the crowd listening to Jesus as He delivered His Sermon on the Mount were no doubt hearing truths that shocked, confused, challenged, and compelled them.

3. Invite a third volunteer to take a seat and read Matthew 5:10-11 aloud. Guide the group to highlight the descriptive words in the passage. Inquire whether words like *persecuted, insulted, lied about*, and *evil* evoke happy feelings or other. Again point to Jesus's extraordinary insistence on turning what, on its face, seems so negative into a positive. Question: **How easy or difficult is it for you to rejoice under this kind of pressure? What can you do to withstand it with the right attitude?** Dig deeper into the topic of persecution of Christians. Talk about the promise of rewards in heaven.

Point out that as followers of Jesus, at some point in our Christian walk, we will suffer as Jesus did. Note that while very few of us will be called upon to give up our physical lives and no one suffers all the time, one of the marks of following Jesus is becoming a target of people who oppose your message and who may damage your reputation, threaten your self-esteem, destroy your livelihood, defriend or isolate you, and more. Encourage the group to think about such episodes as a special time of communion with Christ. Point out that those who suffer for Christ's sake are amassing rewards in heaven, which should bring comfort. Ask a volunteer to read Psalm 34:18, which reveals that God draws close to the brokenhearted and saves those crushed in spirit. Invite the group to reflect on how in their times of suffering, they've felt closer to God.

4. Call on a fourth volunteer to take a seat and read Matthew 5:13-16. Guide the group to highlight the two primary words in the passage: *salt* and *light*. Note that these are two metaphors that are intended to illustrate how blessed Christians live in the world. Invite the group to compare their emotional responses to these two terms: **Does salt evoke as much of a positive as light?** Break down the two concepts and their application for living.

Draw attention to PSG, page 24 where the writer suggests that these two terms should not be considered separately but as a whole. Discuss the idea that we must actively serve as both salt and light. Talk about what happens if a Christian presents only as salt or only as light. Also take some time for the group to identify ways that Jesus showed Himself as salt and light—at the same time. Point to His conversation with Martha when He affirmed Mary and gently showed Martha the better way (Luke 10:38-42), or how He carefully confronted the woman at the well (John 4), acting as salt to help her identify sin while shining the light of God's love.

YOUR NOTES

THE GREATER RIGHTEOUSNESS OF THE KINGDOM

Before the Session:

a. Review Matthew 5:17-48 from the Bible. Make a list of the subjects that Jesus defined for His audience. Circle the phrase, "But I tell you"—or some variation of it—each time it appears in the passage.

b. Read chapter 2 in the Personal Study Guide as well as the related Expository Notes in this Leader Guide.

c. Gather Personal Study Guides, extra Bibles, and pens for the group. Have available **Teaching Item 5: Sermon on the Mount Illustration** if you choose to display again. Download to print or project **Teaching Item 6: Hard Topics Discussion Starters** and **Teaching Item 7: The Truth about Divorce**.

d. Pray for the group who will be engaged in the January Bible Study.

Leading the Session:

1. Introduce the session by sharing **Teaching Item 5: Hard Topics Discussion Starters**. Depending on the size of your group, divide the large group into three to six teams to discuss questions related to anger, adultery, divorce, oaths, charity, or treatment of enemies. Instruct groups to spend a few minutes on their question and appoint a team leader to report back to the large group on the most common or interesting responses.

After giving each group a few minutes to discuss, introduce the study by noting there are topics that we immediately recognize as challenging and there are also topics that we sometimes fail to recognize as challenging until we give them thorough consideration. Direct the group to the opening paragraph PSG page 26 to discover the tough question that the writer asks and briefly discuss.

Point out that all of the questions already discussed during the session have some relevance to Jesus's preaching in the Sermon on the Mount. Remind the group that the Scripture passage will be a continuation of the sermon that Jesus shared with an audience of disciples and seekers. Review the setting for the Sermon: Jesus, on a mountain, sitting down, surrounded by a throng of people hanging on every word. You may choose to display **Teaching Item 4: Sermon on the Mount Location** again for those who were not at the first session.

Enlist two volunteers who will help read the Scripture passages during the session. Instruct the two volunteers to read verses 17-20 in tandem with the first person reading until the second person chimes in on all lines that begin with "I tell you" or similar phrase. Quiz the group on the initial guidance communicated by the first speaker as well as the deeper insights provided by the second reader. Note that in the first set of verses, Matthew 5:17-20, Jesus addresses the question that the writer asked: Do Old Testament teachings still apply in New Testament times? Ask: **Based upon Jesus's words here, how would you answer that question?** Encourage the group to discuss

YOUR NOTES

what it means for the law to remain intact but also for Jesus to fulfill it. Direct the group to PSG page 30 for a fuller discussion on what fulfillment signifies in this passage. Compare the least in the kingdom of God with the great, according to the passage. Highlight verse 20 where Jesus says our righteousness should surpass that of scribes and Pharisees. Lead the group to a deeper understanding of what this means with a simple question: **What did the righteousness of the scribes and Pharisees look like? Is it something to be emulated?** Call on a volunteer to read Matthew 23:23 for deeper insight.

2. Call on your two volunteers to read Matthew 5:21-26 in tandem, with the first reader again reserving the "I tell you" statements for the second reader in order to highlight the expanded insights Jesus offered His listeners. Note that the writer points out in the PSG that most people would conclude that the act of murder is evil—but perhaps stop short at understanding its relationship to anger. Talk about the practical advice that Jesus offers in the passage, such as a definition of defamation or encouraging us to take the initiative to settle out of court instead of putting yourself in a judge's hands. Move on to discuss the spiritual implications found in the verses: how contempt for someone else is a repudiation of the command to love others as yourself or how it nullifies any other gift to God, who demands reconciliation first.

3. Direct your two readers to move to the next part of the passage and read Matthew 5:27-30 in the same manner as before. Compare Jesus's instruction on adultery and lust and compare it to His teachings on murder and anger. Note that in both cases, Jesus directed His listeners from an external, consequential action to the heart attitude that led to it. Inquire: **This is another hard topic. Should we be considered guilty for an internal thought that did not lead to the external action? What's the difference between temptation to sin and the sin itself?** Encourage the group to define the words *temptation* and *lust*. Note that there may be a fine line between the two, but attention to the Holy Spirit, who convicts us of sin, will help us identify it. Draw attention to Jesus's shocking encouragement to cut out one's own eye or chop off a hand if that helps one control a wayward impulse. Invite the group to consider whether this is practical or spiritual counsel. Direct them to the **Cut it Out** activity in their PSG to consider practical ways to apply this passage.

4. Call on your readers to recite verses 31-32 to learn Jesus's teachings on divorce. Note that Jesus was attempting to move His listeners beyond the legalities of divorce to get to the hard heart of the matter. Take a few minutes to talk about the history of divorce from a biblical perspective, utilizing **Teaching Item 7: The Truth about Divorce**. Guide the group to review each of the Bible verses on their own and then volunteer their takeaways from the readings. Ask: **Understanding that we live in a culture of divorce, when we add in the unintended consequences of adultery compounded by more adultery that Jesus talked about, how does that make you feel?**

5. Invite your volunteers to read verses 33-37, once again taking turns to highlight the "I tell you" statement. Emphasize that Jesus's words challenge us to make certain our own words are true. Call on another volunteer to read James 1:19-20, drawing attention to the "slow to speak" instruction. Invite the group to share times when they made ill-advised vows or spoke hastily out of turn. Reinforce that Jesus is telling us to be judicious with our words and weigh them carefully.

YOUR NOTES

6. Guide your readers to recite verses 38-42 with emphasis on the "I tell you" truths. Point out that as hard as the previous teachings have been, here Jesus took His listeners into even deeper waters. Encourage the group to break down what it means to turn the cheek or go the extra mile. Note that while these are familiar phrases, they also may be alien behaviors. Ask: How does the ideal of justice coexist with Jesus's teachings about not resisting an evildoer? Is there a difference between standing up for the oppressed and demanding one's own rights? Encourage the group to consider biblical examples of standing up for the oppressed, such as Moses, and willingly sacrificing one's own rights for spiritual impact as Jesus did.

7. Call on the two volunteers to read the rest of the passage, verses 43-48, in the same manner as before. Lead the group to consider how the act of prayer has both practical and spiritual benefits as we put faith into action in a way that begins to help us rid ourselves of the feelings that prevent us from seeing our enemy as a person made in God's image. Point out that how we treat our enemies is a true indicator of our faith and perseverance as a Christian. Ask: **How do you test yourself in this? If you have mastered the art of nonretaliation, have you also mastered the art of extending love instead? Or have you settled for ignoring your enemy?** Lead the group to discuss how to stay safe from an enemy's attack while also extending love. Suggest that in His wisdom, Jesus offered the act of prayer as a critical solution. Invite the group to share any personal examples of times when they were able to extend love to an enemy. Examine the courage that may have been required or any pain involved as well as the rewards of yielding to Christ's command in this matter.

Close the session by focusing on Jesus's admonition in the final verse of the passage by asking: How are we really supposed to be perfect like God the Father? What in the world did Jesus mean by this hard saying? Direct the group to PSG page 31 for an understanding of how the word perfect should be interpreted. Draw the distinction between being sinless and being dedicated to completeness and maturity.

Direct the group to the **Truth and Dare** activity in the PSG, page 38, as a simple way to evaluate oneself on how easy it is to accept—and apply—Jesus's hard teachings. Once they have completed the activity, direct the group to pair up with a partner to review the entire passage together and discuss the "I tell you" statement that most challenged or inspired them to live up to Jesus's words. Encourage the partners to pray for one another as a blessing and benediction.

YOUR NOTES

OUR PRAISE PROBLEM

Before the Session:

a. Review Matthew 6:1-21 from the Bible. Circle the word *don't* each time you come across it in context of Jesus warning His audience about behaviors that serve to pervert righteousness. Underline the word reward each time you read it.

b. Read Chapter 3 in the Personal Study Guide as well as the related Expository Notes in this Leader Guide.

c. Gather Personal Study Guides, extra Bibles, and pens for the group.

d. Print or project **Teaching Item 8: The Lord's Prayer** for use during the session.

e. Pray for the group who will be engaged in the January Bible Study.

Leading the Session:

1. Introduce the session by directing the group to silently read the opening paragraphs, labeled **Our Praise Problem**, page 42 in the PSG. Once group members have completed the assignment, inquire: **Do you agree? Do you think human beings struggle to find the right balance for praise? Do they covet it when they should not, fail to share it—especially with God—when they should, or struggle to keep their own egos in check while either intentionally or inadvertently eclipsing God?** Encourage the group to share personal stories on their challenges in giving God the glory rather than stealing it for themselves. Be prepared to relate a personal example from your own life. To build upon this opening, guide the group to complete the **Upending Praise** exercise in PSG, page 51.

Turn the group's attention to the session's opening verse in the continuing study of the Sermon on the Mount. Call on a volunteer to read Matthew 6:1. Note the PSG point that this verse is a good lead-in and overview of the entire passage to be studied, although subsequent verses will serve to break down and apply that theme. Invite the group to identify at a high level the two primary concepts in the verse: that righteousness should not be practiced for praise of men because it preempts the reward one would get later in heaven. Remark: **For the record, according to this verse, righteousness indeed has its rewards—just not the kind for which so many people settle.**

Say: **To understand this better, let's break down this verse, beginning with a basic understanding of righteousness, which is a prevailing theme of the Sermon on the Mount. First, how would you define it?** Encourage the group to scan the PSG page 45, **Closer Look—Righteousness** for cues on how to define. Challenge the group to scan the section and call out five quick facts related to the concept.

Lead the group to explore and determine that a theme of Jesus's famed Sermon on the Mount is to help His audience define righteousness in its truest sense. Point out that in the context of this verse, He is again impressing it is less about outward trappings than inner motivation. Note, however, His use of the term *practice* in conjunction with righteousness, which means that there is a discipline to righteousness and a reward, but we must choose the kind of reward we seek. Stress that Jesus encourages us to forego the earthly for the heavenly. Say: **Let's think about this another way. What short-term rewards do you often forego in order to achieve long-term goals?** Be prepared to suggest skipping eating out to save money for a vacation or exercising regularly to stay heart healthy, etc. Note that in much the same way Jesus was leading His disciples to seek lasting rather than temporal rewards.

2. Call on a volunteer to read Matthew 6:2-4. Note that Jesus followed His statement about not practicing righteousness in front of others for its own reward with some concrete examples for application. Explain that Jesus employed a series of "don'ts" to clearly communicate how not to practice righteousness in front of others. Ask the group to identify the first example (giving to the poor). Direct them to find the first "don't" in the passage and to describe what not to do with charitable giving. Note that, according to Jesus, trumpeting one's charitable giving actually signifies hypocrisy, not concern for the poor, revealing a deceptive kind of duplicity. Ask: **What is their reward?** (applause). Invite the group to identify the next "don't" in the passage: not letting the left hand know what the right hand is doing. Talk about what this may look like in application when it comes to giving an offering at church, supporting a charity, or helping a friend. Discuss the pressure one may feel to participate in and set an example for supporting, for example, a building campaign. Ask: **How should we balance these conflicting demands?** Encourage the group to brainstorm the concept of secret giving in the context of the rewards we seek.

3. Invite a volunteer to read Matthew 6:6-8. Inquire: **By a show of hands, how many of you remember ever being impressed, inspired, intimidated, or downright turned off by the way someone prayed in public?** Encourage the group to break down their feelings and try to identify what generated them; in some incidents, for example, they may be inspired by someone else's obviously intimate relationship with God. Expand on that by reminding the group that it is dangerously easy to start praying for an audience instead of engaging in a heartfelt conversation with God during public prayer. Note that for the second time in the session study, Jesus compared those who practice righteousness publicly to hypocrites. Direct the group's attention to the word *love* in the context of the verse, noting that such people seek or relish these types of opportunities. Remind the group that Jesus employed a stark term rather than a gentle one to help disciples recognize the potentially duplicitous nature of praying in public to be heard by other people. Link the reward for that to attention, whether positive or negative.

Direct the group to identify another "don't" in the passage (don't babble) and to talk about what that means. Note that the "many words" that Jesus referenced may be religious, intellectual, or even mindless. Point out that Jesus compared people who prayed like this to Gentiles, a striking reminder that these were people who may not even have had a relationship with Jesus yet. Focus on the final truth of the passage, Jesus already knows what they need before it is put into words. Share the point of prayer: communing with and having a relationship with God.

4. Call on the group to recite Matthew 6:9-13, the Lord's Prayer, from

YOUR NOTES

memory together and then read aloud verses 14-15 as a conclusion. Distribute **Teaching Item 8: The Lord's Prayer,** noting that these are familiar words to most people. Give the group a few minutes with the sheet, then invite the group to draw attention to any insights or nuances gleaned from reading and comparing the various translations. Remind the group that while many people, followers of Jesus or those outside of Christ, may be familiar with the prayer and have committed it to memory, taking it to heart is critical. Invite the group to use the guidance from the PSG page 48 to dissect the prayer into two vertical and horizontal parts, the petitions directed at the heavenly realm and those directed at the earthly. Point to the heart of the Lord's prayer, the desire to bring heaven to earth. Draw attention to the final two verses in the passage, noting that their application does bring heaven to earth as we accept God's forgiveness through Jesus Christ and extend and model that same opportunity with others.

5. Direct the group to read Matthew 6:16-18 silently in their Bibles. Note that this is the third example and set of instructions on how not to practice righteousness. Lead them to find the "don't" in this passage. Talk about whether the group is familiar with the practice of fasting or practices it, noting that this was a routine practice in Bible times. Direct the group to complete the **Lost Art of Fasting** activity, PSG page 49, to educate them on the practice. Discuss the validity of fasting today, which is typically understood as forsaking food and drink as Jesus did in the Bible. Be prepared to compare it to more contemporary understanding of fasting, such as Lent or giving up certain other activities to spend more time in prayer and focus on God. Note that whatever we abstain from in order to be more devoted to God also should be a private practice, not a pronouncement or proclamation if we want a reward from God rather than an earthly one.

6. Invite the volunteer who read the opening verses to read Matthew 6:19-21, noting that just as Matthew 6:1 was a perfect lead-in to the session, these verses are a perfect conclusion. Ask the group to identify the "don't" in this passage (don't store up treasures on earth). Highlight the word *treasures*, pointing out that another word that could be used—and was used throughout the session—was *rewards*. Point out that once again Jesus emphasized that short-term rewards that we allow to satisfy us wear out, waste away, or may be stolen from us while we can be confident that heavenly rewards are the opposite: valuable and permanent.

THE BRIDGE TO WHOLENESS

YOUR NOTES

Before the Session:

a. Review Matthew 6:19-34 from the Bible. Pay attention to the numerous things Jesus employs to make His points. Make a list of the items. Once you have completed this preparation, be prepared to transfer your list to **Teaching Item 9: The Sermon and its Symbols Sheet** as a master study guide to use with the group.

b. Read chapter 4 in the Personal Study Guide as well as the related Expository Notes in this Leader Guide.

c. Gather Personal Study Guides, extra Bibles, and pens for the group.

d. Print **Teaching Item 9: The Sermons and its Symbols Sheet** and make copies for the group to use during the session.

e. Pray for the group who will be engaged in the January Bible Study.

Leading the Session:

1. Greet the group and introduce the session by noting that the study of Jesus's Sermon on the Mount continues in the middle of chapter 6. Invite the group to chime in to provide a quick review of the Sermon themes through the past three sessions. Be prepared to lead them to recall what it means to be blessed and Jesus's teaching on the Beatitudes from Session 1. Briefly note His enlightening insights on hard and hot topics like murder and anger, divorce and adultery, and loving one's enemies, all in the context of true righteousness. Remind the group that the theme of true righteousness, which is threaded throughout the Sermon, also carried over into session 3 with a probing warning of not settling for temporal or earthly rewards when a purer practice of righteousness will yield heavenly or lasting rewards.

Introduce the session theme by sharing an old saying. Comment: **Have you heard this familiar and skeptical piece of advice: "Follow the money"? It's often employed to suggest that the handling of money may be at the heart of many a deceitful scheme.** Note that as distrustful and dubious as that may sound, Jesus crafted the next part of His message on the Sermon of the Mount to follow the money. Say: **The Bible tells us repeatedly that how we handle money and possessions reveals a lot about us.**

Pass out copies or project **Teaching Item 9: The Sermon and its Symbols Sheet** and pens and direct the group to listen for key, highly symbolic words that Jesus used to illustrate His points whenever today's lesson passages are read. Proceed to read aloud Matthew 6:19-21. Inquire whether the group recalls the passage from the last session and point out that these verses are serving double duty by also being used in this session's lesson. In the prior study, the verses served as a conclusion. However, this passage now serves as an introduction to

YOUR NOTES

the current study. Point out that as a master communicator Jesus seamlessly moved from one subject to another but carefully wove a common thread through the whole sermon. Note that throughout the sermon, Jesus often used the term *rewards* to encourage His followers to think about the lasting value of righteousness, but by substituting that term for treasure, He easily moved into a discussion of money and possession. Note that just as throughout the earlier parts of the Sermon, Jesus's goal was to enlighten His audience on what true or whole righteousness—lived out in everyday experience—looks like and to clear up their misconceptions. Inquire of the group which key words they recorded for these verses. Highlight the words *treasure*, *moth*, *rust*, *thieves*, and *heart*. Dwell on the word *heart* and invite the group to consider, like the chicken and the egg question, which comes first, treasure or heart. Ask: **Is it possible to have your heart in the right place but accumulate the wrong kinds of treasure? Will hoarding treasure that is not worthy of Christ eventually serve to corrupt your heart?** Invite the group to share their thoughts.

2. Remind the group to fill in their key words sheet as you read Matthew 6:22-24 aloud. Inquire which words they wrote down from the passage and focus first on *eye*, *lamp*, and *light*. Draw attention to the cultural implications of the eye being the lamp of the body according to the writer highlights, noting that the eye was considered to be akin to a flashlight that shines out with the strength of what is in one's heart. Note that once again, Jesus is encouraging His listeners to understand that our devotion to God and service to Christ should be with a pure, wholehearted faith. Ask: **What do you think Jesus meant when He referred to a deep darkness that emanates from one's own body?**

Move on to the next part of the passage by asking: **Who are the masters that Jesus refers to in verse 24?** Lead the group to talk about the temptation to try to serve two masters, especially in light of the understanding that most people need to work to make a living. Point out that Jesus rejected the idea that it is possible; one will become loved and the other hated. Ask: **So, if we are to serve Christ yet do a good job in our employment without hating it, what are some safeguards or guidelines that we may need to acknowledge and put in place to prevent our work from getting the upper hand as our master?** Instruct the group to complete the activity **Workplace Goals** on page 57 in the PSG for more insight on how the disciples and other early Christians managed it.

3. Direct the group to continue filling out the **Sermons and its Symbols Sheet** while you read Matthew 6:25-34 aloud. Connect the dots to the earlier discussion by suggesting that Jesus addressed one of the primary and sneaky ways that money takes control of out lives: anxiety. Ask: **By a show of hands, how many of you have ever felt anxious about how to pay a bill, a job loss, or struggled with getting ahead in life financially, even if for all the right reasons: to provide for your family, to assist others through charity, and so forth.** Point out that Jesus understood this very real feeling but also took care to try to help His listeners understand that such anxiety stems from a lack of understanding. Draw attention to the word *worry* and invite the group to decide, based upon this verse alone, whether it is acceptable as a Christian to become anxious about finances. Ask: **Why or why not?** Note that Jesus was calling His disciples to a higher level of faith and trust in God, not just with their finances but in all of life. Direct the group to page 59 in their PSG for more research on why we should not worry.

Beyond that, point to the specific examples that Jesus used in the passage, beginning with a focus on life that goes well beyond food, drink, and clothing. Say: **Perhaps you have heard it said that too many of us live to eat rather than eat to live. Most of us spend a great deal of time and effort on the task of putting food on the table and clothes in the closet. Why would Jesus point out that that these are essentially inconsequential activities?** Direct the group to read John 10:10b and draw the conclusion that Jesus wants our lives to be much more fulfilling than a pursuit for the next meal. Remind the group of Jesus's instructions on how to pray, covered in the prior session in the Lord's prayer, that took into account our concern about our next meal and prescribed the proper method for dealing with it. Guide the group to complete the **No Worries** activity in their PSG. Summarize: **You have been made privy to the secret through the exercise you just completed. It's not striving for more or worrying about where and how to get it—it's taking that request to God, daily, and trusting Him.**

Invite the group to share whether they wrote down birds and flowers on their listening guide. Point out that both are deeply appreciated creations. Note that some people pursue birding avidly and travel across the globe to catch sight of a rare bird. Suggest that probably everyone in the room either enjoys growing or receiving flowers, and yet even if they are birders or flower enthusiasts, they don't have to worry about the well-being of these creations, just enjoy them. Link these examples to Jesus's reminder that God did something wonderful in that creation and takes care of them and will do more for human beings. Point out that Jesus directly challenged His disciples on this point by asking where their faith was. Ask: **Why does Jesus remind us that God knows what we need? How does that make you feel?**

Suggest that conventional wisdom is that it's easier to give up a negative attitude or habit if we simultaneously replace it with something positive. Note that Jesus does that for His listeners in the sermon: He tells them to seek first the kingdom of God and His righteousness with the promise that all of the rest, those necessary but mundane things of life, will be theirs, too.

Close the session by drawing attention to verse 34 and ask: What are your worries today? Invite the group to share and pray for them. Encourage them as they leave to let tomorrow and its worries take care of itself. Say: **How do we do that? We pray tomorrow, too.**

YOUR NOTES

YOUR NOTES

THE RIGHT WAY TO JUDGE

Before the Session:

a. Review Matthew 7:1-12 from the Bible. As you read, note the sets of congruencies or couplets and draw arrows between them.

b. Read chapter 5 in the Personal Study Guide as well as the related Expository Notes in this Leader Guide.

c. Gather Personal Study Guides, extra Bibles, and pens for the group.

d. Print **Teaching Item 11: You Be the Judge** and make several copies for use during the session.

e. Pray for the group who will be engaged in the January Bible Study.

Leading the Session:

1. Greet the group and introduce the session by noting that you will pick up the study of Jesus's Sermon on the Mount with chapter 7 in Matthew. Note that today's session begins with Jesus's teachings on judging others. Invite the group to share top-of-mind impressions when they think about the role of a judge. Note that depending on one's personal experiences, one's impressions may be either positive or negative. Talk about the traits or characteristics they would like to see in someone who assumes or accepts the role of judge.

2. Read Matthew 7:1-2, noting that these verses may be a familiar passage to many Christians. Point out the congruencies in the passage that you recorded during your preliminary study: don't judge = won't be judged; judge by the same standard = judged by the same standard; measure = measured. Say: **But we need to clearly understand what Jesus meant when He employed the word *judge*.** Point out that the PSG brings some insight to the passage which may give the group a deeper understanding. Direct the group to divide into subsets of smaller groups and provide each with a copy of **Teaching Item 11: You Be the Judge.** Divide the list of words on the page and assign a subset to each group. Direct the group to examine their assigned words, each of which may potentially serve as a synonym for the word *judge*, in light of the passage and consider whether the synonym is congruent in meaning and conveys what Jesus intended. Note ahead of time that some words may be applicable and others not. When the groups complete their task, invite them to call out the words they considered would double for judge as well as the words they discarded. Ask for explanations of why they chose or rejected a word. Affirm that the exercise shows that the word ***judge*** in the passage may be more nuanced than one may assume at first glance.

Draw attention to PSG page 69 and invite a volunteer to read biblical scholar R. T. France's quote as well as Scot McKnight's quote. Ask: **If there is a place in civil society and, more to the point, Christian living for evaluating the behavior and actions of others as safeguards for living in peace and harmony, how important is it to avoid a harsh or critical spirit? Where does mercy enter the picture?** For further amplification, call on volunteers to read James 2:12-13 and James 4:11-12 aloud.

YOUR NOTES

3. Transition to Matthew 7:3-6 and read the verses aloud to the group. Note that these verses provide a compelling—and somewhat comical—visual portrayal of Jesus's caution about inappropriate judging. Compare the splinter and beam examples, noting the irony of ignoring a log in one's own eye to attend to a speck in someone else's. Ask: **How many of you have had the unfortunate experience of trying to remove a splinter with a pair of tweezers? How would a plank in your eye—or even an eyelash that's making you blink—inhibit your ability to perform such an intricate maneuver?** Drive home the point, however, that by directing His audience to first extract an impurity that not only blinds but cripples, Jesus then releases us and deems us capable of helping someone else deal with their issues. Point out, however, that once we have focused on our own shortcomings that others' no longer loom as large.

Highlight the word *hypocrite*, reminding the group that Jesus employed this word several times during the Sermon to emphasize that righteousness dictates that inner thoughts and attitudes must align with external behavior. Direct the group's attention to page 72 in the PSG, Closer Look at Hypocrisy. Turn the group's attention to the metaphors that Jesus used in verse 6, noting that this verse may seem more challenging to understand without additional context. Point to the use of the words *dogs* and *pigs* as terms of contempt and note the warning not to waste the holy or precious on them. Connect this concept to the idea of balance. Just as one must not unfairly judge others or, in congruence, be judged by the same standard, one also must not become the opposite, undiscerning and, in the process, also lose track of the sacred.

4. Move to the next set of verses by calling on a volunteer to read Matthew 7:7-11. Guide the group to again find the congruencies in the passage as you write them on a white board: ask = receive; seek = find; knock = door opened. Ask: **I don't need a show of hands on this, but how many of you find this passage difficult to understand? How many of you find it challenging to put into practice at times? Why?** Encourage the group to share reasons why they may fail to simply go to the Father for assistance and support. Be prepared to guide them to consider lack of a relationship, temptation to worry instead, independence or spirit of pride, unfamiliarity with the process, and so forth. Guide the group to complete the **They Asked He Answered** activity on page 75 in their PSG to reinforce the lesson that God has the power and willingness to supply what we need or want but may choose to wait for us to ask to release His power on our behalf.

To further drive home the point ask a volunteer to read 1 John 5:14-15 aloud and talk about the exercise that the group just completed in their PSG. Ask: **Was confidence a factor in the prayers that you just studied?** Call on another volunteer to read James 1:5-8 aloud. Note that in this case James was referring to a specific request for wisdom but confidence remains a significant factor. Press home that point by suggesting that confidence is required because it demonstrates a genuine faith in God.

Turn the group's attention back to verses 9-11 and point out that Jesus was directing His listeners to put their trust in their Father, just as children trust their parents because, from birth on, they depend on them. Highlight Jesus's point that most parents do their best to provide good gifts to their

YOUR NOTES

children. Suggest that Jesus's words are also an acknowledgement that sometimes they fail, too—yet He assured us that God the Father never lets us down. Draw attention to Jesus's use of the word *evil* to describe His disciples, highlighting that while most of us give ourselves high marks for our parenting skills, Jesus did not pull any punches: in comparison to God our righteousness is like filthy rags; we are evil.

5. Read verse 12 aloud. Note that this verse is commonly referred to as the Golden Rule. Call on a volunteer to also read Luke 6:31, which is another way Jesus stated the same concept at a different teaching time. Call on volunteers to also read aloud Galatians 5:14 and Romans 13:8, pointing out that the apostle Paul also affirmed this teaching. Point out that the Golden Rule supports Jesus's summation of the second part of the great commandment, which represents a summation of the Ten Commandments. Call on a volunteer to read Matthew 22:37-38 to clarify this connection.

Draw attention to PSG page 76 where readers are encouraged to reconsider the Golden Rule as a Golden Vision. Lead the group into a practical application of what this vision may look like in contemporary life. Discuss contemporary cultural implications of a society struggling to be sensitive and empathetic to the feelings of others, including what many consider to be marginalized populations, without condoning sinful choices. Talk about guidelines for common decency that we should extend to all human beings, including civility and mutual respect. Lead the group to decide on their personal expectations for affirmation of human dignity and their ability to extend those same regards to others, no matter their social or spiritual condition. Ask: **Are there any expectations for ourselves that we would not apply to others? What if we put that the other way around? Are there any expectations for the treatment of others that we would not want for ourselves?**

Direct the group to complete the exercise **Refining Gold** on page 77 of the PSG. Invite the group to share any statements that gave them pause and steer them to try to understand whether their hesitancy is godly or from the flesh. Connect the Golden Rule back to the larger teaching of the session and the Sermon on the Mount. Stress that this final verse of the session ties back to the understanding that we should employ fairness in our assessment of others because no one wants to be treated unfairly. Likewise, note that this verse and the session passage all link to the overarching theme of the Sermon, which is focused on helping Christians develop righteousness beyond external behavior to get to the heart.

TWO WAYS OF LIVING

YOUR NOTES

Before the Session:

a. Review Matthew 7:13–8:1 from the Bible. Take note of the sharply drawn metaphors used in the session passage.

b. Read chapter 6 in the Personal Study Guide as well as the related Expository Notes in this Leader Guide.

c. Gather Personal Study Guides, extra Bibles, and pens for the group.

d. Print **Teaching Item 12: Metaphors in the Bible** and make several copies for use during the session.

e. Pray for the group who will be engaged in the January Bible Study.

Leading the Session:

1. Greet the group and introduce the session by noting that you will complete the January Bible Study and study of the Sermon during the session. Conduct a review of the Sermon by asking the group for insights gained from prior sessions.

Transition into the session topic by noting that today's lesson passage is heavy on metaphors. Offer a definition of metaphor as the use of a word, phrase, or image to substitute for another in order to bring more clarity to the subject. Note that some metaphors are very practical and workmanlike while others may be very poetic ways of approaching a subject. Direct the group to listen and try to identify the metaphors Jesus employed in this section of the Sermon on the Mount as you read Matthew 7:13-29 aloud. Outline the three metaphor passages briefly as an introduction to the session passage and elaborate on the meaning of metaphors through **Teaching Item 12: Metaphors in the Bible**. Divide the group to work in pairs to discover some of the other most well-known and loved metaphors found in the Bible. Invite the group to share other biblical metaphors with which they may also be familiar.

2. Break down the passage, beginning with Matthew 7:13-14. Note that, as already stated, the first metaphor Jesus employed in this passage to get His point across was a gate/road. Highlight that the gate and road are described as an option of either narrow or wide but point out that Jesus did not offer a choice without direction. Instead, He guided His listeners to the narrow gate with the word *enter*, which constituted a command rather than a suggestion. Point out that the meaning of a narrow gate and path versus a broad gate and path is very straightforward: the wide easy-to-tread road beckons and looks appealing so a lot of people readily choose it. Stress that in directing Christians to a narrow path, Jesus emphasized that it's not as popular and, on the surface, certainly looks less appealing—but Jesus taught that it is not about looks. The difference in destinations from each option is important and stands in sharp contrast: destruction or life. Acquaint the group with some other insights on the use of the word *path* as a metaphor by calling on a couple of volunteers to read Proverbs 4:18 and Isaiah 40:3. Stress, however, that Jesus specified in this passage that the

YOUR NOTES

narrow path is a difficult one. Sketch your own metaphor by suggesting that the group think of it as mountain hike. Say: **When the longest trail is also the steepest and most challenging, what keeps you going? Why would you encourage someone else to take that trail rather than the easier one?** Encourage the group to share experiences where the promise of reaching the best rock, peak, scenic overlook, waterfall, and so forth made the hike worthwhile.

Guide the group to consider the word *difficult* in the context of this passage. Suggest that the idea of persecution of the saints is a theme of the Bible and Christianity that Jesus and other writers of the Bible did not try to sugarcoat. Point out that someone who serves Christ can expect persecution in the form of criticism or worse. Note that even if it does not rise to undisguised enmity, most Christians recognize that their attitudes and beliefs are usually so countercultural that they experience discomfort and feelings of alienation. Refer to Jesus's earlier metaphor that Christians are to be salt and light, noting that there is a certain amount of duress involved even in these roles. Point the group to PSG page 83 that suggests the difficult work of looking inside our hearts and letting God do a deeper work there.

Tell the group that this excellent metaphor reminds you of Robert Frost's poem, "The Road Not Taken," the tale of a traveler who considered two paths and eventually chose the one with less traffic. Quote the final words of the poem: "Two roads diverged in a wood, and I—I took the one less traveled by, and that has made all the difference."[1]

3. Dig deeper into Matthew 7:15-23 by directing the group read the passage again to identify two intertwining metaphors in the next passage: wolves in sheep's clothing and good and bad trees. Guide the group to dissect these two conflicting metaphors by tracing first one and then the other. Start with the wolf in sheep's clothing metaphor, which symbolizes the false prophet. Note that Christians are often described as sheep in the Bible so a false prophet in sheep's clothing would first appear to be one of them, a friendly and harmless soul. Highlight, however, that Jesus described such a person as a wolf, and a ravaging one at that. Point out that in the childhood tale *Little Red Riding Hood*, while Little Red Riding Hood is initially hoodwinked by this animal dressed up as her grandmother, the reader quickly realized that this was not someone to be trusted.[2] Point out that in His account, Jesus compared the false prophet to a wolf who also eventually reveals its true self—through its fruit.

Note that instead of sticking purely with the wolf metaphor, Jesus switched gears and moved quickly to weave another symbol into His narrative: good and bad trees. Draw the group's attention to the idea that good pickings such as apples and figs could not be produced by thornbushes and thistles. Ask: **Would you expect a false prophet to produce good or bad fruit?** Point to the clarity of the idea that good trees produce good fruit while it is impossible for a bad tree to do that. Highlight that bad trees are eventually cut down and burned. Suggest that it should then be easy to make a simple deduction: **False prophets are like bad trees. They cannot produce good fruit.** Repeat verse 20: "So you'll recognize them by their fruit."

Say: **Or will you?** Call on a volunteer to recite verses 21-23 again. Ask: **What's the fruit that we are to recognize?** Lead the group to discuss how someone may pray

YOUR NOTES

to God, teach His Word, prophesy, drive out demons, and perform miracles in His name—but still not know Him. Inquire: **If such behaviors have all the earmarks of good fruit, how are we to recognize a false prophet?** Lead the group to underline the phrase "one who does the will of my Father in heaven" (v. 21). Stress that the works of a false prophet may replicate works of God—until they don't. Conclude that the role of the Christian is to be discerning and to look beyond flashy antics to detect the true substance of the prophet's heart. This same quality is one that Jesus called for earlier in His Sermon with His expectation that His followers judge with fairness. Ask: **Do you get the sense that the false prophet—and others like him—who tried to make a case that his behavior was evidence of identity with Christ, was surprised by Jesus's flat rejection? If there's a danger that any of us may settle for focusing on outward behaviors without doing the hard work of delving into our hearts, what can we do about it?**

4. Move to the final verses by asking the group to identify the last metaphor of the passage. Discuss the symbolism of the wise man, the house on the rock, and treacherous weather and compare those to the foolish man and house built on sand. Identify the common denominator for these two types of people: rain fell on both. Point back to 5:45, a verse already covered earlier in the study, and invite a volunteer to review it aloud for the group.

Suggest that the failure to undertake the painstaking task of building on solid rock ultimately defeated the builder and revealed a heart condition: foolishness. Call on a volunteer to read Psalm 14:1 aloud. Point out that such foolishness is not a mental or intellectual deficit but a problem of the heart because Christians are not to rely on traditions and laws but the guidance that comes through an intimate relationship with a divine God. Ask: **What then is wisdom? How does the Bible define it?** Lead the group to work **Wise Words** on page 90 of their PSG.

Draw attention to PSG, page 80, where the writer compares Psalm 1 to Matthew 7:13-27 in the Sermon and instruct them to read the section and then work on the **Copying Psalm 1** activity on page 82, PSG.

5. Draw the study to a conclusion by reviewing verses 7:28-29 and 8:1. Note that the Sermon on the Mount was an eye-opening break from rabbinic teaching, a call to give more attention to the inner man than the outer trappings of religion. Highlight that Jesus's listeners recognized that no matter how astonishing or challenging His teachings, Jesus taught as someone who knew His subject. Say: **He knew God and He also knew what was in men's hearts—and it resonated.** Point out that coming down from that mountaintop, Jesus amassed a following. Note that what He said then still applies now.

1. Robert Frost, "The Road Not Taken," *Mountain Interval* (New York: Henry Holt and Company, 1916), 9.
2. Jacob Grimm and Whilhelm Grimm, trans. Margaret Hunt, with introduction by Ken Mondschein, *Grimm's Complete Fairy Tales* (San Diego: Canterbury Classics, 2011), 96.

EXPOSITORY NOTES

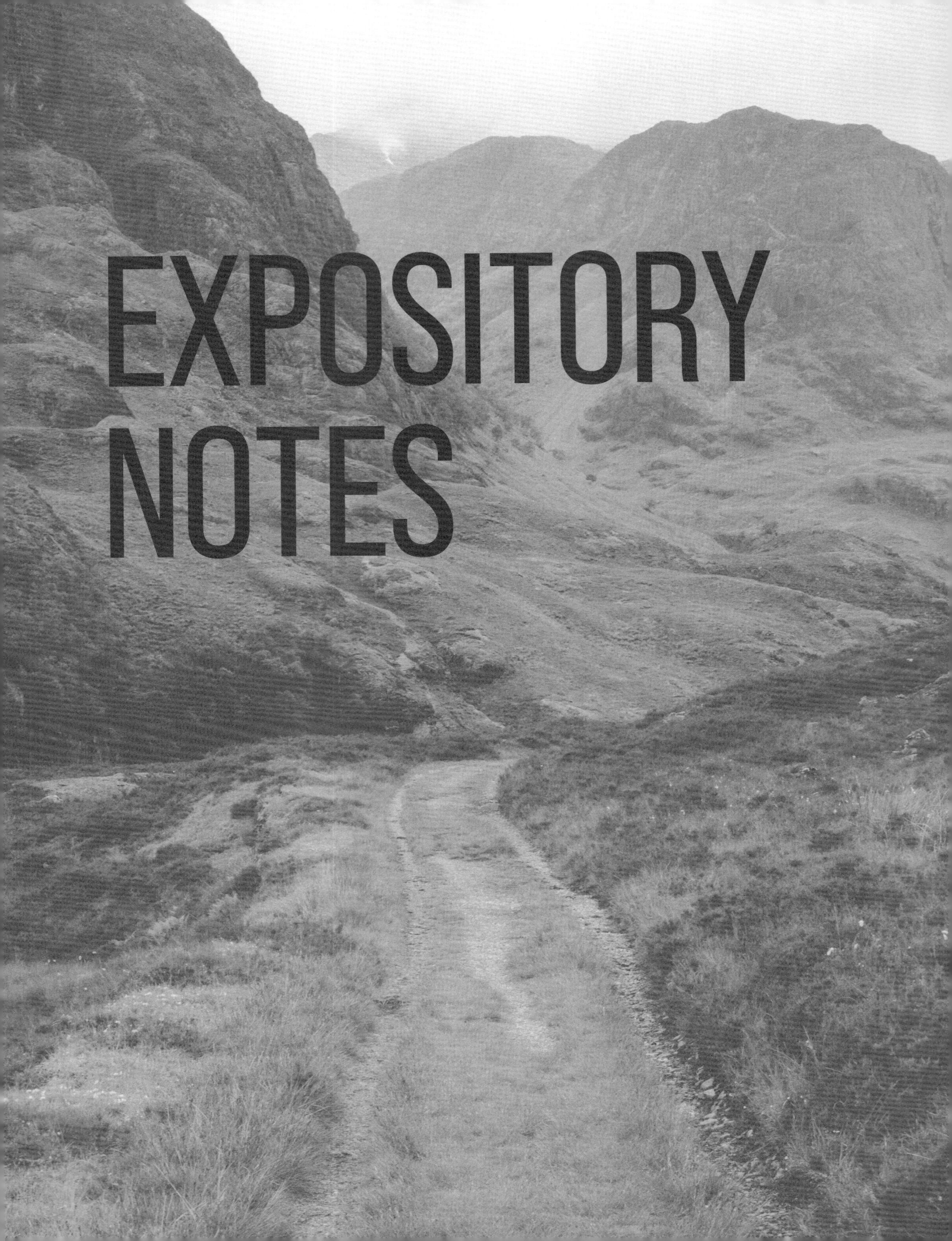

YOUR NOTES

INTRODUCTION TO THE SERMON ON THE MOUNT

For as long as the Bible has been studied, Matthew 5–7 has been a critical passage of Scripture for followers of Jesus. Growing disciples have turned to it for centuries so they could learn more about how to grow spiritually as His disciples. The passage has come to be called the Sermon on the Mount, and it is appreciated as a most remarkable message because of the profound depth as well as the simplicity of the instruction. Knowing the biblical context, the Teacher and the disciples, and the challenges will help to prepare us for our study of this enriching portion of God's Word.

The Biblical Context

The context of Matthew 5–7 brings into consideration the connection of the passage with the Old Testament and the New Testament. The Sermon on the Mount has deep roots in the Old Testament. For instance, the setting as well as the content of Matthew 5–7 bears a striking resemblance to Exodus 19–20. According to that segment of the Exodus account, God called Moses to join Him on Mount Sinai. God instructed him up to the mountain not long after the miracle at the Red Sea. God parted the water of the Red Sea so He could deliver His people from Egyptian bondage to safety and the beginning of their journey to the land of Israel. With the miracle still fresh in his mind, Moses ascended the mountain. There, God instructed him about the law that He intended for His people to embrace as they followed Him. He expected them to keep His law as they made their way to the Promised Land. Also, He intended for them to live according to His law once they settled there. On the mountain, Moses received the Ten Commandments and the accompanying law. With God's law in hand, Moses made his way back down the mountain to lead God's people so they would affirm their devotion to Him and His ways.

The setting for the Sermon on the Mount looked quite similar to the Exodus account of God's people at Mount Sinai. Jesus called His disciples to join Him on a mountain. Identifying which mountain has been difficult. However, understanding what Jesus wanted to do with His disciples on the mountain has not been hard to understand. There He intended to teach them that He had come to fulfill the law that God gave to Moses. Jesus instructed His disciples regarding how He expected them to live as they followed Him. After Jesus finished His instruction, His disciples followed Him down the mountain to put what He had taught them into practice as they served Him throughout their lives.

Of course, the New Testament provides enriching contextual information about the Sermon on the Mount too. The context provided by Matthew has always proven to be most helpful. In his Gospel account, he placed the Sermon on the Mount at a time not too long after Jesus began His public ministry. Jesus called four fishermen to follow Him as disciples (Matthew 4:18-22), and they followed Him as He preached the gospel throughout Galilee.

YOUR NOTES

As He preached, others followed Jesus as His disciples. When the time came for Him to give more focused attention to teaching His disciples, Jesus led them to the mountain so He could instruct them.

Matthew wrote his Gospel account in order to show Jewish people that Jesus fulfilled the Old Testament prophecies regarding the Messiah. With the genealogy of Jesus, for instance, Matthew sought to validate the Jewish linkage between He and Abraham (Matthew 1). From there, He isolated significant Old Testament prophecies that were fulfilled with His birth, His baptism, and His ministry (Matthew 1–4). In the same way, Matthew recorded what Jesus said in the Sermon on the Mount about coming in order to fulfill the Old Testament law (Matthew 5:17-19).

Portions of what Jesus taught in Mathew 5–7 found their way into other segments of the New Testament. For example, overlap of the Sermon on the Mount can be seen in the instruction of Jesus in Luke 6:12-49. According to that passage, Jesus had chosen His twelve disciples. After choosing them, He led them and many other disciples to an open plain, and He instructed them there. Some of the precepts He shared with them on the plain echoed the instruction He had given on the mountain.

Other New Testament writers showed the influence of the Sermon on the Mount in their letters to churches. James included allusions to it often in his epistle to a church that had been scattered (James 1:2-22; 2:5-13; 4:4-12). In Peter's epistle, he called attention to the Sermon as he encouraged believers to live for Christ as they faced persecution (1 Peter 2:12; 3:13-14; 4:14).

The Teacher and His Disciples

The setting of Matthew 5-7 included the Teacher and His disciples who joined Him on the mountain. Of course, the Teacher is Jesus, the Savior who provided the way of salvation. His birth, life, ministry, death, and resurrection fulfilled the Old Testament prophesies about Messiah. Jesus set out on His messianic mission by proclaiming the gospel, driving demons out of their victims, and healing sick and disabled people everywhere He went (Matthew 4:23-24). Throughout His ministry, He never lost sight of His mission to provide the only way possible for anyone to receive the gift of eternal life. His preaching focused on the kingdom of God. The miracles He performed in His messianic mission validated the message of good news that He preached.

Large crowds kept growing as people from everywhere came to Him. Along the way, people devoted themselves to Him as His disciples. Peter, Andrew, James, and John were the first of His disciples. Early in His ministry, He called them to follow Him (Matthew 4:18-22). Later, He chose the other followers to compose the band of twelve disciples. They followed Him everywhere He went. In due time, He sent them on mission to people living in Jewish regions. He sent them under His authority and with specific instructions (Matthew 10:1-23). Luke recorded that Jesus sent out seventy-two disciples to minister under His authority and in keeping with His messianic mission (Luke 10:1-12).

As Jesus led His disciples, He made teaching them a priority in His ministry. The Sermon on the Mount was one of many settings in which He taught them about being His disciples.

YOUR NOTES

After His ascension, they would be responsible for bearing witness to Him in their world (Acts 1:8). He instructed them before His crucifixion so they would be prepared to bear witness to Him after His resurrection. For example, He taught them about the challenges and rewards of discipleship (Matthew 10:24-42) and explained how He used parables in His instruction (Matthew 13:1-23). These and other teaching opportunities with His disciples had either an implicit or explicit connection with the Sermon on the Mount. Taken together, they reflect the value that Jesus placed on teaching His disciples then and how we are to live for Him now.

The Challenge

As we take a closer look at Matthew 5–7, we will be given the opportunity to join the first-century disciples and learn from Jesus. As we delve into these chapters of Scripture, we will encounter the following themes: authentic happiness for a disciple, what's really inside a disciple's heart, the reward of being a disciple, a disciple's attention to spiritual disciplines, a disciple's spiritual eyesight, and the need for a disciple to practice discernment. After engaging in the instruction of Jesus in keeping with these themes, we'll be presented with the challenge to grow as His disciples in our world. Accepting that challenge involves entering the narrow gate, making wise fruit inspections, and choosing to build our lives on the rock. As we take a closer look at the Sermon on the Mount, we can be assured that the Teacher will take a closer look at us. The world in which we live leaves us with no other choice than to grow toward maturity in Christ. Taking the Sermon on the Mount seriously by applying it to ourselves will help us to live out that wise choice. By making such a choice, we'll see that the lifelong journey of discipleship is the only way to be genuinely happy in Him.

YOUR NOTES

JESUS'S (SHOCKING) VISION FOR THE TRULY BLESSED LIFE

Most kids like to get new sneakers, but some of them want their shoes to fit well. For that reason, they plead with their parents to make sure that the shoes they buy aren't too big for their feet. Of course, parents respond to their child's appeal in a variety of ways. Likewise, their responses may change as they become more experienced parents. With their first child, for example, parents may try diligently to get their hands on sneakers that fit just right. However, as other children come along, parents may respond to the appeal with less of an eagerness to seek precision in the foot-to-sneaker dilemma. They may tell their son that even though the sneakers may be a little large right now, he will grow into them in due time.

Does growing into the sneakers involve surgery? Does it mean that their son will need to take a course on how to grow his feet? Will he be required to change his diet so his feet will grow into his new shoes? Of course not. His feet will grow into his sneakers as he grows as a child. One day he will find that his shoes fit his feet perfectly. And he will be happy.

Becoming a loyal disciple means embracing the qualities that Jesus brings us at the beginning of the Sermon on the Mount. Like a child grows into his shoes, disciples grow into the qualities of discipleship by growing up in Christ. As we grow into them, we find ourselves happy in Him.

The Source of Spiritual Happiness (5:1-2)

Jesus had become quite popular by the time He took His disciples on the mountain for what has been called the Sermon on the Mount. **The crowds** had been gathering ever since He began His public ministry. He had gone from the wilderness in which He had been tempted by the devil to the Galilean region, and He stayed in Capernaum. The city would become a central location in His ministry in Galilee as He began to preach the message about the need to repent. He proclaimed that the kingdom of heaven had "come near" (Matthew 4:17). Along with preaching, He began calling His disciples. Matthew named Andrew, Peter, James, and John were some of His first disciples. Following Jesus, they and the other disciples who would join them had the opportunity to observe as He continued to preach a message of repentance, heal people who were sick, and drive demons out of their victims.

News about Jesus had spread far and wide, and growing crowds gathered to be with Him. They came from everywhere. Of course, Galileans gravitated toward Him, but so did people from Jerusalem and the region of Judea. Surprisingly, even folks who lived in the Gentile area called the Decapolis came to be with Him, and they were joined by others who came from as far away as the eastern side of the Jordan River (Matthew 4:23-25).

The growing crowds probably consisted of a wide variety of hearers. Some of them were eager listeners who would become loyal followers in the years ahead. They may have known

YOUR NOTES

about His Jewish roots, and they came to learn from Him about His perception of the right path to take in order to live as God's people. At the same time, people with no Jewish background at all came to be with Him too. Some of them came out of interest in His message, while others simply wanted to be healed. They didn't know anything about His messianic mission, but they knew that He had a reputation for healing sick or disabled individuals. These people were often accompanied by friends and other loved ones who desperately wanted to see them healed. While they had confidence that Jesus could heal, they had no perception of His mission to provide the way of salvation so they could enjoy the gift of eternal life. They did not have a clue about His relationship with God, His Father. Likewise, the notion that He was God the Son may not have crossed their minds.

People who doubted Jesus could be seen in the crowds too. The Jewish leaders in those days consisted of groups like the Pharisees, the Sadducees, and the scribes. They had taken on the responsibility of developing Jewish laws that would guide the nation of Israel to be God's people who would follow Him with loyalty and purity. They also served as enforcers of the Jewish laws they had established. They enforced these laws with heavy hands. Accordingly, they always kept their eyes open for Jewish people who were breaking the laws and for anyone who would threaten their authority. For that reason, they begun to pay attention to Jesus. The effectiveness of His preaching ministry and His reputation as a healer had started to make them uncomfortable, so they joined in with the crowds to listen to Him, but they listened to Him in order to confront Him when He broke their laws or appeared to be too popular.

Others who doubted Him also joined the crowds. As a result of the heavy-handed religious pressure that had been placed on them by the Jewish leaders, they had become cynical. They wanted to know how to have a relationship with God, but they weren't very interested in becoming more religious. They longed to hear a message that had the ring of truth. That's why they came to be with Jesus. They could tell that He seemed to be different, and His message appeared to be relevant. They wanted to observe Him more, so they joined the large and growing crowds, but at a distance.

Of course, He often found His disciples in the crowds. These people had given themselves to Him, and were eager to follow Him everywhere He went. However, their eagerness to follow Him was often accompanied by a lack of understanding of His mission and their role in fulfilling it. They had much to learn, but Jesus was ready **to teach** them.

No one knows for sure which mountainside Jesus chose as the site of the Sermon. The Galilean landscape provided places in which a teacher could sit and teach his disciples and be heard by a large gathering of others who had come to listen. Neither does anyone really know how long He taught them after He led them there. But of note to Matthew was that Jesus **sat down** to teach. In those days, teachers sat when they taught, and their disciples would gather around them to listen and to learn. As Jesus commenced with His instruction, everyone in the crowd received the remarkable blessing of hearing what He said. For the individuals who came for reasons that had nothing to do with His messianic mission, what Jesus said may have been lost on them. But what He taught would be central to the spiritual growth of His disciples, both present and future.

YOUR NOTES

Happy in our Relationship with God (5:3-6)

The mountainside that has been identified as the possible site where Jesus taught His disciples has come to be called the Mount of Beatitudes. The Latin word for "Beatitudes" means blessings. Instructions about blessings for God's people can be found in the Old Testament. For example, the first verse in Psalm 1 introduces the certainty of being blessed. The psalmist referred to the blessing in terms of what would make a person "happy" (1:1). Along with "happy," the Greek word for "blessed" could also carry the idea of being fortunate, and it could bring to mind the picture of someone being congratulated. If we choose to speak of being blessed as being happy, the Beatitudes provide us with the qualities that would render lasting happiness in our walk with the Lord. These qualities include poverty, comfort, humility, and satisfaction.

Poverty (5:3)

Jesus begins His instruction by telling His disciples that they will be happy once they acknowledge that they are spiritually impoverished. Being **poor in spirit** brought into view the prevailing understanding about poverty in those days. People who lived in poverty were completely powerless, so they had no way of improving their difficult circumstances. For that reason, no one wanted to be impoverished. A miserable life of poverty would force a person to abandon any morsel of pride. Instead of being proud, their constant shame over being poor would keep them humble.

Jesus points to our need to be powerless with His instruction about being spiritual paupers. We're humbled when we reckon with the certainty that our efforts to make ourselves spiritually rich before God will always be futile. Our sin separates us from intimacy with Him (Romans 3:23). Because of our sin, we're helpless when it comes to doing something on our own that would remove it. Participating in countless rituals and keeping endless rules does nothing to turn God's head and compel Him to take away our sin. The only way to be right with God is to be to recognize our need to repent of our sin and seek His forgiveness. When we take that important step, the door of the **kingdom of heaven** opens to us.

Comfort (5:4)

Jesus goes on to instruct His disciples about what happens when we come to terms with our spiritual poverty. We **mourn** over our spiritual condition. We're spiritual paupers, and we're helpless to do anything about our sin. The confession of the Old Testament prophet Isaiah comes to mind when we ponder our sinful condition. Like Isaiah, we lament that we're sinners who have "unclean lips" (Isaiah 6:5). Furthermore, we live among others who share in the same spiritual poverty because of personal sin. No longer can we ignore it or laugh it away. Our sin becomes detestable to us, and we want to get rid of the guilt associated with it. For that reason, we turn to the Lord empty-handed and ask Him to forgive us.

YOUR NOTES

When we turn to Him in repentance, we're **comforted** with the blessing of His forgiveness. Our sorrow over our sin gives way to spiritual relief that gives way to contentment in our relationship with Him. Jesus used the same word for "comforted" (*parakeleo*) when He taught His disciples about the Holy Spirit (John 14:16,26; 15:26; 16:7). When we repent, the Holy Spirit comforts us as we turn to the Lord and seek His forgiveness. For maturing disciples, nothing brings more happiness than knowing that He has forgiven us and embraced us in His love.

Humility (5:5)

Humility in our walk with the Lord nourishes spiritual happiness in our lives as we follow Him. The word **humble** can also be translated as "meek" (ESV) or "gentle" (NASB). These words bring to mind someone who is characterized by self-control and restraint. However, the Greek word (*praus*) for being humble in this verse does not imply being weak. Rather, it portrays disciples as followers of the Lord who have decided to place their trust in Him instead of themselves. In the days of Jesus, pagan leaders frowned on such humility. They thought that only a strong, aggressive, and harsh person would be victorious. In stark contrast, Jesus taught that a disciple demonstrated self-controlling humility by trusting Him. In fact, He personified that kind of humility Himself. He encourages those who come to Him to see He is "humble in heart" (Matthew 11:29).

Disciples who live in humility get to experience the spiritual happiness that comes with inheriting **the earth**. As God's people traveled through the wilderness after their exodus from Egypt, they looked forward to inheriting the promised land in keeping with His promise. Likewise, the disciples of Jesus trust Him completely to provide everything necessary to live out His intention for us. In addition, we live in the certainty that in eternity we will enjoy the inheritance of a "new heaven and a new earth" (Revelation 21:1).

Satisfaction (5:6)

If we intend to be happy in our walk with Jesus, we do well to consider His wisdom about satisfying our spiritual **hunger** and our **thirst**. People who have no interest in following Jesus tend to devote themselves to satisfying the longings in their lives in ways that have nothing to do with Him. As a result, their yearnings are never satisfied completely. As growing disciples, we yearn to grow in our walk with the Lord. Instead of being right in our own eyes, we want nothing more than to be upright in His eyes. He alone made us righteous by saving us from our sin and giving us new life in Him. We're eager to grow into the righteousness that He's given us as our highest priority. When we give ourselves to Him in that way we experience the unique kind of abiding happiness that He alone can give. This is the happiness that accompanies fulfillment. In other words, we're **filled** with complete and lasting satisfaction. As we follow Him, nothing makes us happier than growing toward maturity in His righteousness.

YOUR NOTES

Happiness in Our Relationships with Others (5:7-12)

Later in his Gospel, Matthew wrote about a Jewish leader who asked Jesus to share the greatest commandment. Jesus responded by declaring that loving God with everything that's in us and loving our neighbors like we love ourselves serve as the greatest commandments of all (Matthew 22:36-40). The so-called Great Commandment prompts us to love Him by loving others. Therefore, our relationship with Him has an effect on our relationships with people. As Jesus continues to teach maturing disciples about being happy in our walk with Him, He brings the truth of the commandment into view. After showing His disciples the qualities of happiness that emanate from our walk with God, He turns our attention to the qualities of happiness in Him that can be seen in our relationships with others—we're merciful, our hearts are pure, and we serve as peacemakers. Finally, we expect to be persecuted.

Being Merciful (5:7)

Jesus describes disciples who are walking in spiritual happiness in their walk with Him as **merciful**. Mercy has to do with not giving people what they deserve. A disciple's merciful behavior reflects positively on God's endless mercy (Lamentations 3:22). His mercy toward us has no end because of His tremendous love for us, even when we were dead spiritually and eternally because of our sins (Ephesians 2:4-5). Following the example set by our Lord, we demonstrate that we're growing as disciples by extending the mercy He has shown us to others. The desire to show mercy fills our hearts with empathy because we have taken the time to put ourselves in the place of the people who need us to be merciful toward them. As we put mercy to work, we agree with James, who wrote that "mercy triumphs over judgment" (James 2:13).

Our happiness over being merciful comes from the awareness that we will be **shown mercy**. The connection between the mercy we show others and the mercy we're shown does not mean that we're merciful to others so we can earn God's mercy for ourselves. We know that God's mercy toward us comes from His love for us. We don't show mercy in the hope that we'll receive mercy. Instead, we're merciful to others because we know for certain that God's mercy has been extended to us through our faith in Christ. Therefore, the blessing of His mercy fills us with happiness in Him.

Having a Pure Heart (5:8)

As Jesus turns our attention to disciples who are **pure in heart**, He opens the door to the exploration of our motives for serving Him. A pure heart comes from inspecting our motives to avoid doing something for a reason that doesn't please the Lord. Consequently, having a pure heart requires us to get rid of hidden agendas and secretly malicious motivations for our actions. Disciples who have pure hearts want nothing more than to honor the Lord and please Him in every action that we take and every word that we speak.

YOUR NOTES

Serious disciples who embrace this Christ-centered quality of a pure heart enjoy the happiness that comes with seeing **God**. Granted, seeing Him doesn't only mean that we will one day actually look upon Him in person, though we will. It also implies that we **see** God at work all around us. Every day we become more aware of His presence in our lives. Such a perspective distinguishes us from people whose hearts are filled with self-centered motives. As they seek to please nobody but themselves, they tend to look for evil all around them, and they usually see it everywhere. We see what we look for in life. Pure hearts see God at work because we're looking for Him so we can enjoy His presence.

Being a Peacemaker (5:9)

In our relationships with others that flow from our walk with Jesus, we're growing in Him when we experience lasting happiness by being **peacemakers**. The term "peacemakers" appears only in this verse. It's not used anywhere else in the Bible. However, Paul assures us that God took the initiative to reconcile us to Himself. Reconciliation came when Jesus made peace between God and us on the cross (Colossians 1:19-20). Therefore, the miracle of peacemaking can only be attributed to Jesus. Our role as peacemaker involves pointing people to Him so they can experience the peace He alone can offer. Consequently, a maturing disciple lives to share the good news of Christ so others can experience peace with God through Him. For believers, peace involves contentment and fulfillment because we've been made right with God.

When we point people to Christ so they can experience peace with Him for themselves, we enjoy the blessing of being seen as God's children. Our identity as disciples who belong to the Lord becomes a source of happiness for us.

Expecting Persecution (5:10-12)

Jesus assures His disciples that we can enjoy happiness in Him even though we have to deal with negative reactions to our determination to embrace Him and His ways in our lives. Persecution will come our way because we have taken the path of **righteousness** that centers on Him, and we reflect this in our relationships with others. As we face persecution, we live in the certainty that the kingdom of heaven is our home and that we'll live there for eternity in due time. Such a spiritual certainty enables us to endure persecution. Jesus provides us with some of the ways in which we can count on being persecuted. He warned us that we may be insulted, or we might be the objects of false accusations. We can rest assured that evil efforts will be made to silence us simply because we belong to Him. The history of the church has validated the warning of persecution that Jesus gave His disciples.

Although persecution may be difficult to bear, we can **be glad** at the same time. Our joy in the face of mistreatment comes from the certainty of our **reward** once we get to heaven. He assures us that it will be **great**. Words cannot express the rewarding blessing of being in the presence of Jesus that awaits us. Jesus also encourages us to keep in mind that

YOUR NOTES

when persecution comes our way, we're in the notable company of **the prophets** who faced mistreatment and remained faithful to Him.

The Influence of a Happy Disciple (5:13-16)

Jesus shifts the focus of His instruction from preparing His disciples for persecution to helping us grasp the reach of our influence in the world. Taken together, the two focal points drive home the same important challenge. The disciples of Jesus have the responsibility for making a difference in the world, especially when we face persecution. He describes the influence that His disciples can have in the world in terms of salt and light. By using these two word pictures, He gives us a couple of lasting images to embrace as we grow in Him.

Being Salt (5:13)

People living in the days of the Bible used **salt** to season their food and to preserve it. The quality of preserving food made salt a symbol of covenants for God's people (Numbers 18:19; 2 Chronicles 13:5). Jesus's word picture works well to portray the glaring difference between His disciples and the world around them.

Food that was not covered in salt eventually decayed into a rotting heap. However, salt added to food prevented it from deteriorating. By the same token, the world in which the disciples of Jesus had been placed had to endure the harsh reality of moral decay because of the constant spiritual corruption brought on by sin. Jesus intended for His disciples to have a positive influence in the world.

Who we are as His disciples guides our thoughts, words, and actions. By being a faithful disciple of Christ, we have the potential for making a monumental difference. Of course, our influence has limits. Salt cannot transform something that's rotting into something that's thriving, but it could keep decay from spreading without restraint. In the same way, only Christ can transform a person who is overcome by spiritual decay into a someone who is thriving spiritually. However, we can make a difference as His disciples by halting the spread of moral and spiritual decay as we live for Him in our world.

Salt can lose its ability to preserve food. In the days of Jesus, impure salt could become tasteless when the sodium chloride leeched out of it. When that happened, salt became worthless. Because it served no other purpose, it was **thrown out.** Jesus's comment about throwing out tasteless salt did not imply that His disciples could lose their salvation. However, they could lose their usefulness.

Being Light (5:14-16)

YOUR NOTES

Everyone who listened to Jesus as He instructed His disciples about their influence on others knew that darkness could only be driven out by the light. When Jesus used light as a word picture to describe the influence of His disciples in their world, He provided them with a simple but profound way to understand their value.

His instruction to His disciples then continues to resonate with growing believers now. We understand that the world lives in spiritual darkness and that it can be driven out only by the light of Christ. He compels us to embrace the potential influence that we have as **the light of the world**. At the same time, we embrace the truth that He's "the light of the world" (John 8:12). Our role as light has nothing to do with being His understudy. We don't see ourselves as His substitutes. Instead of shedding our own light, we simply reflect His light through our lives. This word picture encourages us to see our role in shedding light that drives out the darkness by comparing it with the light shed by moon and the sun. The moon has no light of its own. It shines at night because it reflects the light of the sun. Similarly, disciples reflect the light of Christ through our lives so others can see Him at work through us. At the same time, this helpful word picture compels us to understand that we don't merely reflect the light of Christ. It actually shines from within us. As we allow Him to transform us into His image, His light shines in our hearts and our minds, and it becomes evident in our actions. In that way, we don't need to force His light to shine through us in what we do in our world. We simply allow His light to shine through us by being who we are as His disciples.

When we see our roles in the world in that way, we live in the certainty that the light of Christ shines through us. We become like a **city** situated at the top of a **hill** that glistens with a brilliant glow. The light punches a huge hole in the darkness of the night. Also, we're like a **lamp** that's burning in order to shed light in a **house.** Nobody would think about lighting a lamp only to cover it with a **basket**. Similarly, our **good works** that emanate from our enlightened hearts and minds are intended to shed light on our heavenly **Father** and glorify Him. By being who we are as His disciples, we point people to Him. Therefore, we can't hide our devotion to Him from the world around us. We display our happiness in Him by letting His light shine though us.

YOUR NOTES

THE GREATER RIGHTEOUSNESS OF THE KINGDOM

Suppose you're in the market for a house. You've located a possibility, so you make an appointment to explore it. When you arrive at the property, you notice that the lawn has been well manicured. The flowers have been cared for, and they're showing their health with the beautiful colors they're displaying in the sunlight. The front door of the house looks just as appealing. Once you make your way through the door, however, you observe that the previous owners did not pay much attention to the inside of the house at all. You make your observation based on the rancid smell, the dirty floor, the broken cabinet doors, and the leaking refrigerator.

As Jesus continues to help believers grow toward maturity in discipleship, He teaches us about His mission and how He wants us to live in keeping with it. His instruction also involves the need for us to understand that our spiritual growth begins in our hearts. If we only focus our energy solely on keeping religious rules and observing routine rituals, we may look like we're spiritually mature. However, we're missing the true fulfillment that comes with growing as His disciples from the inside out.

Fulfilling Instead of Abolishing (5:17-20)

After Jesus introduces the qualities of happiness for His disciples, He goes on to clarify His role in the world. In order to account for the perspective of His disciples regarding His mission, He takes them to the Scriptures. As He moves them to a clearer grasp of His messianic role, He clears the air regarding what they should **not think** about Him. He starts by telling them what He would be doing as He carries out His mission. He left them with no possibility of misinterpreting Him or His ministry. With straightforward simplicity, He assures them that He did not come in order **to abolish** the Scripture. The Greek word for "abolish" (*katalyo*) conveys the idea of doing away with something or destroying it. In the days of Jesus, God's people had the Old Testament. It provided them with **Law**, which took up the first five books. It also included the **Prophets**, the other books in the Old Testament. Taken together, the Old Testament related the account of how God led His people to take His Word seriously so they would live according to His ways. Jesus declares that He has no intention to do away with the Scripture. Throughout His ministry, He registers the highest regard for God's Word.

Jesus challenges His disciples who listen to His instruction to remember what He said about the Scripture. For at least some of them, the Old Testament had been the source of the long list of tedious laws that weighed them with heavy religious burdens. Those laws had been developed and enforced by the Jewish leaders. But Jesus's challenge left His disciples no reason whatsoever to think that He would abolish the Scripture.

Jesus validates the declaration of His unqualified devotion to God's Word by asserting that He had come to **fulfill** it. Matthew used the same word in the previous chapters of His

YOUR NOTES

Gospel account to underscore the reality that prophecies in the Old Testament had been fulfilled in Jesus. In Matthew 1:22-23, for example, he noted that the virgin birth of Jesus had fulfilled Isaiah's prophecy (Isaiah 7:14). Similarly, in Matthew 2:5-6, he wrote that the birth of Jesus in Bethlehem fulfilled the prophecy of Micah 5:2. He went on to declare in Matthew 4:14-16 that when Jesus moved to Capernaum, He fulfilled Isaiah's prophecy (Isaiah 9:1-2). Jesus declares the truth that Matthew affirmed. He came to fulfill the Scripture, which included the completion of His messianic mission in keeping with God's redemptive work that had been declared in the Old Testament. Of course, fulfillment of the prophesies of God's Word also included the truth of His second coming.

But Jesus didn't stop there. He also exclaims emphatically that God's Word would endure until the passing of **heaven and earth**. Furthermore, He declares His commitment to the complete authority of Scripture by pointing to the **smallest letter** as well as the **stroke of a letter** in the Hebrew alphabet. Even though those letters appeared to be insignificant, they mattered to Him. By pointing out their value, Jesus exhibits His high regard for the Scripture. He did not come in order to cast God's Word aside to be forgotten. Instead, He would never waver in His certainty that God would accomplish everything that He said in His Word.

By saying **therefore**, Jesus turns the attention of His disciples to God's people who would be living out the precepts of His Word. He shares a solemn warning for anyone who determined that they could simply abandon God's Word. In the process He refers to the Scripture as **these commands**. Of course, the Old Testament had the Ten Commandments, and God's people knew them well. The Old Testament also contained other commands that God gave in accordance with the Ten Commandments. In addition, the Old Testament signified God's commands in the historical account of His ways with His people, the wisdom literature that accompanied it, and the prophetic utterances that had been preserved in it.

Jesus's solemn warning resonates with disciples of every generation. From time to time, His people may be tempted to break His commands, perhaps because they are considered to be somewhat meaningless. To break His commands means to set them aside. By setting them aside, even though they may be seemingly insignificant, believers make a foolish mistake. We're mistaken if we think that we can decide which portions of God's Word deserve our attention. Even worse, we do an injustice to growing Christians who entrust us to teach them how to embrace and live out God's Word. When we teach them that they can cherry pick the parts of the Bible they want to embrace and reject the portions that appear to be unsavory to them, we will be held accountable for what we have done. According to Jesus, we'll be considered the **least** in **the kingdom** that centers in Him. However, maturing disciples who take every portion of God's Word seriously are recognized in a positive way. When we determine that we will live by God's Word and teach other believers by the precepts we share and the example we set, we have the honor of being respected as **great**.

Once more, Jesus becomes emphatic in His instruction. His glaring exclamation has to do with **righteousness.** By bringing up the need to be righteous, He points to the necessity of being right with God and then living in a way that would be seen as upright in His eyes. What Jesus said next to His disciples must have jolted them. He tells them that if they are not righteous, they will not enter the **kingdom of heaven**. His declaration challenges them

YOUR NOTES

to grasp the importance of righteousness as they follow Him. Jesus links it to their spiritual destiny. However, what He said about the **scribes and Pharisees** must have also shocked them, at least at first. He tells His disciples in no uncertain terms that their righteousness has to **surpass** the uprightness embraced by these revered Jewish leaders. They had a reputation for keeping the Jewish laws flawlessly, and they expected the people of Israel to be just as faultless in their attempts to keep them.

The emphatic exclamation of Jesus can trouble believers today too. Even though we haven't encountered the Jewish leaders Jesus mentioned, we know enough about them to come to be troubled by His assertion. Nobody can out-Pharisee a Pharisee, and nobody would ever be able to out-scribe a scribe.

We're relieved and challenged at the same time when we consider what Jesus has to say about what's important in being righteousness. In the instruction of Jesus that follows, we begin to see what righteousness looks like to Him. He gives us six examples of superlative righteousness at work in the relationships we nourish with God and others. These examples help us to understand that righteousness that pleases the Lord starts on the inside. From there, it can be seen on the outside.

Being Righteous (5:21-48)

Each of the following examples share one important detail in common. This detail enables us to see the difference between righteousness on the inside and righteousness on the outside. When we think about righteousness on the inside, we have in mind what's happening in our hearts. However, when we consider righteousness on the outside, we take into consideration certain actions that we consider to be important. At the beginning of each example, Jesus points to the difference when He distinguishes between what others have taught us and what He intends to teach us. In each example, what others have taught us focuses our thoughts on religious actions, but what He teaches us helps us to examine our hearts.

Anger (5:21-26)

Jesus teaches His disciples about what they have **heard** from their **ancestors** regarding the sixth of the Ten Commandments (Exodus 20:13). Obviously, Jesus points to the Jewish leaders who considered **murder** to be a sin and a crime, and they affirmed that murderers needed to face **judgment**. When they murdered someone, they sinned. However, if they never committed homicide, then they were free from the guilt associated with murder.

Jesus underscores that breaking the sixth commandment starts with what happens in the heart before it becomes a crime. He teaches that the sin of murder begins inside people when they harbor anger in their hearts. Their simmering anger eventually leads them to **judgment**. Likewise, their smoldering anger provokes them to insult their spiritual siblings. Jesus considers such a disgusting action to be worthy of accountability to a **council**. Brooding anger in a person's heart is the driving force underneath the sin of hurling hateful names

YOUR NOTES

like **fool**, moron, and imbecile at someone else. People who call others such cruel names deserve the judgement of **hellfire**. The Greek word (*Gehanna*) for "hellfire" called to mind the garbage pit south of Jerusalem in which the bodies of executed criminals would be burned. According to Jesus, harsh judgment awaits anyone who allows anger to infect their hearts completely. Of course, true repentance always results in merciful forgiveness.

In the face of Jesus's appraisal of anger, we do well to examine our hearts as growing disciples and get rid of anger before it festers into incriminating actions. Jesus provides us with two scenarios in which He shows us the need to get rid of anger. The first scenario involves worship. Unlike first-century disciples who worshiped through **offering** their **gift** at the temple, twenty-first-century believers usually give tithes and offerings in a worship service at church. At the time of the offering in the worship service, when we give back to the Lord in response to everything He's given us, a spiritual sibling in Christ who **has something against** us may be brought to mind. At first, we may choose to ignore the nudge to seek reconciliation. But the need to **reconcile** with our **brother or sister** will not go away. We'll see that we can't present our offering to the Lord wholeheartedly until we have been reconciled with others in His family whose hearts we may have wounded.

The second scenario involves a court setting. Instead of a brother or sister in Christ, the court scenario involves an **adversary** who has a complaint against us. A **settlement** needs to be reached, and we have the choice of reaching it out of court or settling it in the courtroom. Jesus teaches us to keep anger from allowing the relationship that we have with our adversary to escalate into a hostile conflict. Growing disciples do not want to let anger fester into rage. When we refuse to seek resolution to a conflict, we run the risk of making a difficult situation even worse. As a result, we may find ourselves suffering an outcome that would be more painful than we anticipated. The dreadful scenario provided by Jesus involves a **judge**, an **officer**, a **prison**, and being left penniless because we fostered rage in our hearts. We can easily imagine what such a scenario would look like in today's world.

Fidelity (5:27-30)

The next example involves **adultery**. Jesus brings into view the seventh commandment (Exodus 20:14). The commandment left no room for doubt about what it meant, and His disciples had **heard** the Jewish leaders warn them about the sin of adultery. For Jewish leaders and others who ruled over the people of Israel at that time, the focus of attention was on adultery as sinful behavior. When a man had a sexual encounter with a woman other than his wife, he committed a sin because he violated the seventh commandment. By drawing attention exclusively to the sinful behavior, the Jewish leaders nurtured a legalistic perspective regarding the sin. Only the sexual encounter itself qualified as a sin to be avoided. Accordingly, they only considered what happened on the outside of a person. Jesus counters the instruction of the Jewish leaders by telling His disciples that what happens on the inside of a person gives way to the adulterous behavior. Furthermore, He teaches them how to address what is wrong in the heart of a person who will give in to adultery.

YOUR NOTES

Jesus takes His disciples inside a person's heart when He teaches them that adultery does not start with a sexual encounter. Instead, it starts when lust is allowed to be cultivated in a person's heart. Lust could also be referred to as desire, and it takes hold with a look. More than giving a passing glance and then moving on, looking **lustfully** feeds the flame of adulterous intention. Long looks at the object of a person's lust gives way to fantasizing about the possibility as well as the dimensions of a sexual liaison. In turn, adultery is committed in a person's **heart**.

After leading His disciples to recognize that adultery emanated from inside a person, Jesus instructs His disciples about the only remedy for this. He expects growing disciples to take the initiative to remove anything that feeds the flame of adultery in their hearts. Nothing can be considered too sacred to be removed if it plays a role in adulterous behavior. In those days, people considered the **right eye** to be worth far more than the left eye. Jesus must have surprised His disciples when He made no exception for the right eye. The priority of having a pure heart matters most of all to Him. People with hearts full of lust would have no interest in following the directive of Jesus. They would never **gouge out** their right eye and discard it. Because of their rejection of Him, they would keep their eye, but they would be **thrown into hell**. In other words, their lust would consume and eventually destroy them.

When Jesus tells His disciples to cut off their **right hand**, He punctuates the instruction given about the right eye. In His day, the right hand mattered more than the left hand. Therefore, cutting it off would be perceived as a drastic but necessary step so lust would not grow in a person's heart.

Jesus intends for His disciples to take drastic steps to remove anything that feeds the flame of adultery that may be burning in our hearts. He offers no room for exceptions.

Divorce (5:31-32)

Jesus has more to teach about marriage. Some of the marriages among Jewish people ended in divorce. Quite a number of the failed marriages could have been linked to lustful looks that turned into adulterous behavior. He taught His disciples to look inside and deal with the root causes of lust aggressively. Now Jesus gives them instruction about the value of nurturing their marriage relationships. In the process, He demonstrates that marriage involves much more than a contract. Therefore, growing disciples would strengthen their relationships with their spouses. Likewise, they would not allow their marriages to be little more than legal agreements that they could end whenever they wanted.

The disciples who listened to Jesus apparently knew about the prevailing instruction that pertained to divorce. The instruction involved a document called the **written notice of divorce**. Moses mandated it whenever marriages came to an end (Deuteronomy 24:1-4). Men had the freedom to divorce their wives. However, women had no footing for themselves in the community when their husbands decided to divorce them. The written notice served to provide divorced women with an official certification that their marriages had ended. It permitted them to marry again, but it prohibited them from marrying for a second time the husband who had just divorced her.

The mandate of a certification may have helped to give divorced women credibility, but it did not prevent men from treating marriages like contracts that could be broken. For that reason, Jesus became assertive about the way that He intended His disciples to view marriage and divorce. What He mentioned in these verses only briefly, He explained further in Matthew 19:3-12. His assertion goes straight to the inside of a growing disciple by exposing the insufficiency of seeing marriage only as a legal agreement.

He insists that marriages should not be ended hastily. Of course, marriages torn apart by adultery did not fall under His insistence. After affirming the exception regarding adultery, Jesus calls on husbands to see that they are responsible for what they caused their wives to do once they divorced them. They left the wives they divorced few options for fending for themselves. By ending a marriage, husbands ended a relationship that they should have nourished.

YOUR NOTES

Honesty (5:33-37)

As Jesus continues to give His disciples a glimpse into the kind of righteousness that He affirmed, He points out the difference between religious trickery and true honesty. A person who wants to weasel out of an **oath** will lean on trickery, while devoted followers of Jesus will make honesty their priority. Of course, tricksters are content with righteousness on the outside, but growing disciples guard their walk with the Lord by nurturing what's going on inside them spiritually.

The scenario that Jesus provides in His instruction would have been understood by His disciples. They knew that God warned **their ancestors** about taking an oath. When they took an oath, they made a promise to someone in God's presence, which made it binding. An oath made before **the Lord** took the form of a debt to Him that had to be paid. The third commandment underscored the absolute necessity of keeping an oath (Exodus 20:7). Invoking God's name in an oath brought accountability to Him into the picture. Therefore, the oath before God could not be broken, and the promise had to be kept (Numbers 30:2).

Because of the seriousness of taking an oath before the Lord, religious tricksters found ways to make a pledge without invoking His name. As a result, their oaths would turn out not to be binding. They developed an approach to oaths that made most of them not binding at all. They would make a promise and swear by **heaven** that they would keep it. Or they would swear **by the earth** or **by Jerusalem** that they would keep their promise. Of course, such oaths were not binding because God's name had not been brought up in the promise that had been made.

Jesus points to the flaw in the logic underneath the oath-keeping scheme. He points out that every oath brought God into the picture one way or the other. For example, God occupied His **throne** in heaven, and placed His feet on the earth. Therefore, making an oath without bringing up His name still invoked Him because He created everything. Even an oath sworn by a person's **head** invoked the Lord. He alone determined the color of a person's hair.

YOUR NOTES

Instead of making elaborate promises that fudge on credibility, Jesus insists that His disciples practice honesty by keeping their word. Accordingly, our word when we speak serves as our bond. Saying **yes** or **no** alone should be sufficient. Our integrity underscores the certainty that we keep our word. When we determine that we will affirm honesty, we don't give the **evil one** an opportunity to tempt us into trickery.

Retaliation (5:38-42)

In a growing believer's relationship with others, integrity takes first place, and not only when it comes to keeping our word. It also entails how we practice righteousness from the inside out when we face the temptation to retaliate. While we may have the right to retaliate, we choose to take the path of forbearance because of what the Lord is doing in our hearts.

Jesus reminded His disciples of a life principle that they had **heard** and the Old Testament reference that supported it (Exodus 21:24). As Moses led God's people out of Egyptian captivity, he saw that they retaliated in a way that took the form of harsh revenge. For instance, if a man took out someone else's **eye**, then the wounded person would retaliate by killing him. Moses decreed that retaliation could only involve such brutality. A person who lost an eye could take nothing more than the eye of the man who hurt him. Of course, the Jewish leaders interpreted the decree of Moses to justify their practice of retaliation that would give way to revenge.

The disciples of Jesus needed to embrace the truth about retaliation. For that reason, He provides four examples of responses they might make to being injured or mistreated. Their responses would reflect the righteousness in their hearts that He intends for them to nurture. One example included being slapped on the **right cheek**. While being slapped hurt physically, it also harmed a person emotionally. People in those days perceived a slap as a painful insult. Instead of striking back, a growing disciple would **turn the other** cheek in forbearance. Jesus Himself modeled this approach when He asked the Father to forgive the people who were nailing Him on the cross (Luke 23:34).

Another example brings a lawsuit into view. People living in Israel had to contend with harsh weather. Therefore, they wore coats to protect them from heat or cold. A **coat** had life-preserving value, so a person being sued would not be required to surrender it. However, the inner garment, a **shirt**, could be taken. Jesus teaches His disciples to be gracious enough to surrender their coats along with their shirts.

With the other two examples, Jesus urges His disciples to avoid the temptation to retaliate. Going the second mile and being generous with others helps to reinforce His directive to nourish our hearts so we will be gracious, merciful, forgiving, and forbearing.

Love (5:43-48)

YOUR NOTES

The example of living for Jesus from the inside out takes His disciples to the arena of **love**. Jesus directs our attention to the depth of love that He expects us to exhibit in our relationships with people who mistreat or persecute us. He sets His expectation against the backdrop of what had been **said** about loving others.

Jesus leads His disciples to remember what must have been a common refrain. God's Word taught His people to love their neighbors. The basis for the refrain came from passages like Leviticus 19:18. In fact, Jesus quotes this passage as He talked about the Great Commandment (Matthew 22:36-40). However, the Jewish leaders added a statement to what had been written in the Leviticus passage. Their additional statement gave God's people permission to **hate** their **enemies**. Therefore, anyone could exclude their enemies from their list of people they intended to love. Jesus challenges the additional statement that the Jewish leaders included. His challenge leaves His disciples with the necessity of taking a long look in their hearts, the place in which the righteousness that He affirmed would be cultivated.

In a simple but thought-provoking manner, Jesus gives us two reasons for loving our enemies and exhibiting it by praying for our persecutors. First, we want to resemble our **Father in heaven**. He graces **evil** people as well as **good** people with the same demonstration of His love. It comes in the form of the rising **sun** and the refreshing **rain** that benefits everyone everywhere, not just a selected group. Second, we don't want to love so we'll be loved. By mentioning **tax collectors** and **Gentiles**, Jesus brings to mind two groups of people who knew nothing about love being its own reward. If they loved, they expected to be loved in return. Growing disciples choose to love because God's love lives in our hearts. In so doing, we allow our Lord to set the standard for our spiritual maturity.

YOUR NOTES

OUR PRAISE PROBLEM

As Jesus continues to teach us how He expects us to grow as His disciples, He moves us on to another area of our lives that deserves consideration. Throughout His instruction, He has been helping us so we can learn to nourish a relationship with Him that's characterized by true happiness. In doing so, He shows us that authentic righteousness starts in our hearts. He goes on to teach us what that kind of righteousness looks like in our interpersonal relationships. When our spiritual growth in Him begins in our hearts, we express it in healthy relationships with others.

Now Jesus turns our attention from interpersonal relationships to spiritual disciplines. For believers who want to grow from spiritual infancy to maturity in Him, spiritual disciplines play a valuable role. Professional baseball players don't become proficient instantly. They give priority attention to exercising, practicing, and enduring the long hours needed to become excellent. Similarly, mature followers of Christ have learned the value of practicing the spiritual disciples necessary for spiritual growth. Jesus places three spiritual disciplines before us and teaches us how to grow to spiritual maturity through our wholehearted devotion to giving, praying, and fasting.

Giving (6:1-4)

Before Jesus gets us into three spiritual disciplines so we can avoid the hypocrisy of showing off our superior spirituality so others will be impressed with us, He states a life principle for us to embrace, shared as an imperative. Stated in that way, it's much more than a simple instruction. It's more like a stern command. He intends for us to take the initiative when it comes to how we live out our relationship with Him. He expects us to take responsibility for being **careful** to keep a firm grip on our motive for living out our **righteousness**. If we lose our grip, we may be tempted to display the outward indicators of our relationship with God for the wrong purpose. We'll exhibit our righteous behavior only for the purpose of being complimented by someone who's watching us.

Jesus brought up the issue of reward earlier in His instruction. Now He returns to it because it's a central issue in living our walk with Him in public. Do we express our faith publicly so we can be rewarded with accolades from others? Or are we completely satisfied with the reward that we receive from Him?

After Jesus set forth the principle about living out righteousness, He provides three examples of how to put it to work in everyday life. The first example involves the spiritual discipline of giving. He knew that His followers would give to the poor. In the Old Testament, God directed people to keep a compassionate eye on poverty-stricken individuals and families (Deuteronomy 15:11). Throughout the history of Israel, caring about the poor became a part of their culture.

Giving to the poor was woven into the fabric of Judaism. So was the tendency among Jewish leaders to seek the approval of people around them when they made their contributions. For that reason, they liked to "sound a trumpet" or call attention to their offering.

YOUR NOTES

During the days of Jesus, boxes to collect offerings for the needy could be found at the temple. At the top of each box, a copper funnel shaped like the horn on a trumpet was installed. Givers dropped their money down the funnel and into the box. Of course, the funnel made a distinctive racket when the money was dropped into it. Self-righteous hypocrites made lots of noise when they dropped their huge offerings through the funnels. The loud racket would catch everyone's attention. For that reason, Jesus called them hypocrites. In the Greek language, the word (*hupocrites*) painted the picture of an actor on stage. Jesus knew the motive for their giving. They wanted to be rewarded with applause. Indeed, people may have applauded them, but the Lord would not reward them because of their motive for giving.

Maturing disciples of Jesus reflect a different motive for giving. We only care about pleasing the Lord with what we give. We're to be so serious about it that we take precautions so the motive of our offering won't be misconstrued. Jesus helps us grasp the importance of protecting ourselves from being misunderstood with His statement about not letting our left hand know what our right hand does with our gifts. The statement is extreme, and it enables us to see the high priority of keeping a pure motive in view as we give. Our gifts are meant to come from our hearts. We give because we have been moved with the compassion of Christ. We simply want to meet the needs of others. When we give out of such a selfless motive, we enjoy the reward that comes from our heavenly Father. Unlike the applause of others, the spiritual benefit we receive from Him is a reward that never fades away.

As we apply the principle of giving in our present culture, we may develop the notion that a receipt of our tithes and offerings to our church may be inappropriate. We may conclude that we should not have any record of our gifts at all. In our culture, our giving record only helps us with our income tax returns. It's not designed to pat us on the back because we're faithful to the Lord with our resources. When we put the receipt away so nobody except an accountant or an auditor will see it, we're living out the principle of giving in secret.

Praying (6:5-8)

The second example of piety in public involved praying in the presence of others. God's people learned the value of prayer together early on in their relationship with Him. In turn, it became a prevailing feature in their worship culture. When Jesus instructs His disciples about prayer in these verses, He does not suggest that His followers should not **pray** with others or in the presence of them. Rather, He wants them to avoid the temptation to turn public prayer into an opportunity to show off their self-righteous piety. He refers to people who give into such a temptation as **hypocrites**. They pretended to be spiritually mature so others would admire them.

The **synagogues** and the **streets** served as the stage in which the pretenders would act like followers of God with sparkling spiritual superiority. The synagogues where they worshiped with others supplied them with a platform on which they could display their skills of religious pretense. On the streets, they could easily capture the attention of a crowd. When **people** saw them, they paid close attention. When the affirmations came their way,

YOUR NOTES

they got what they had been seeking all along. Obviously, they enjoyed the **reward** that came with being affirmed. Jesus tells His disciples that they would not be rewarded with anything more.

From there, Jesus teaches the best approach to praying. When we take His instruction about praying in a **private room** seriously, we will likely come to appreciate it as our favorite way to pray too. The private room can be a bedroom, a living room, or any other place in which we can be alone with Him. A room without a window would be a choice place for a conversation with Him. Once we **shut** the **door** to the room, we close out the possibility of turning our prayer time into a public spectacle. There, in those private moments with the Lord, we carry on an intimate conversation with Him that enables us to start our day, get through struggles, settle our minds, seek His help, and end our day. Those **secret** moments with Him become the centerpiece of our walk with Him. They **reward** us with spiritual blessings that consistently enrich us. Consequently, we make being alone with Him in prayer a daily priority.

Next, Jesus brings up another bad habit that He wants His disciples to avoid as they pray in the presence of others. This particular example didn't come from Judaism. Instead, the habit could be found among the **Gentiles**. In those days, Jewish people regarded Gentiles as pagans. Their religious practices revealed that they did not know anything about the God of the Old Testament. They prayed, but their prayers were not conversations with the living God. When they prayed to their deities, they babbled on and on with empty words and phrases that sounded like chants and incantations. With their meaningless utterances, they hoped to get the attention of their idols. They had a hunch that if they kept on hurling an endless volley of **words** into the air, their idols would eventually hear and answer them. Therefore, they would work themselves into a frenzy as they repeated worthless syllables without stopping.

We're wise when we distinguish the difference between the frenzied praying of the pagans and sincere intercessory prayer. When we keep on bringing a need to the Lord, we're not engaged in a pagan habit. Quite the opposite, we're following the direction given in Scripture about praying with persistence (1 Samuel 12:23; Matthew 26:44; Romans 12:12).

Jesus refreshes us with His reminder about our **Father**. When we pray, we don't talk to a deity who has to be awakened to our need. We don't have to keep on saying meaningless words to Him in order for Him to realize that we're calling on Him for help. Neither do we need to worry that He has problems with His memory. Our Father does not have to be reminded of our need because He has a troubling tendency to forget about us. Jesus assures us that our Father **knows** what we **need** before we bring our concerns to Him in prayer. Therefore, when we pray, we're not trying to get His attention. We already have His attention because He already knows our needs. In response to the reality that He already knows what we need before we pray, we may question the value of prayer. The answer to the question becomes clear in our conversation with Him. In those moments when we're with Him, He helps to clarify our real need and our motive for asking Him to meet it (James 4:2). He also gives us His wise perspective on our need and His trustworthy response to it. Best of all, He blesses us with His faithful, loving presence as we deal with our need.

Teaching Prayer (6:9-15)

YOUR NOTES

So far in this passage, Jesus has shown us how to spend time with God in prayer so it will be spiritually rewarding. He marks the transition in His instruction with a key word—**therefore**. What Jesus teaches next about how to engage in prayer should not be viewed only as a poem to be memorized. It's more than just an excellent literary contribution. Jesus gives it to us as a model to use as we **pray**. With the guidance of His model, we can grow deeper as we mature in discipleship. We can embrace the important features of our conversation with Him when we pray. As a result, our prayer time with Him, whether brief or extended, will be an enriching experience that will have lasting effects on us as we serve Him.

Jesus shows us how to start by referring to God as **our Father**. Of course, the Bible provides us with a number of titles to use as we talk with God. However, addressing Him as our Father renders the perfect blend of majesty and intimacy as we approach Him. The reference to **heaven** reminds us of God's home, and it's our home too if we belong to Him. At the same time, we remember the honor He deserves because His **name** is set apart completely as **holy**.

Following the guidance that Jesus has given us in His model prayer, we submit to our Father and His plan instead of asking Him to support our plans. We underscore our submission by acknowledging His plan has to do with the coming of His **kingdom**. When we pray in this way, we declare our willingness to obey Him in whatever He directs us to do in keeping with His plan. His kingdom will come **on earth** according to a time frame that He has set **in heaven**. We confess that we anticipate the fulfilment of His plan according to His will and way.

As we wait for the coming of His kingdom, we need resources so we can carry out His plan for us. Jesus teaches us to ask for the resources by referring to them as **our daily bread**. Any number of helpful insights about asking for daily bread have been offered for believers. One insight helps us see the connection between growing disciples and God's people as Moses led them from Egyptian slavery to the promised land. We follow the pattern that God established for His people in the wilderness, we trust Him to provide us with what we need each day (see Exodus 16:4-5). By turning to Him each day to ask Him for what we need, we learn that we find complete satisfaction with what He gives us. This also serves as a prompt to seek Him daily.

Next Jesus turns to our need to pray regularly for forgiveness. Asking God the Father to forgive us cannot be set aside as unimportant. It's a critical issue, and it has a monumental effect on our spiritual development. If we don't deal with our sinful behavior in the presence of our Father, our walk with Him will be impaired. The deep sense of satisfaction that goes along with being forgiven nourishes our time in prayer with intimacy and sincerity.

Jesus teaches us to think about our sins as **debts** that must be paid. We received the gift of salvation because Jesus paid our entire sin debt with His sacrifice on the cross. He separated us from our sins forever. Now that we have been saved, we want to live with our eyes open to the reality that we still struggle with sinful behavior. Instead of pretending that we don't sin or trying to push it out of our minds, we're wise when we confess our sinfulness and seek His forgiveness.

YOUR NOTES

Along with forgiveness, mature followers of Christ turn to Him in prayer and ask Him for His help. The **temptation** to sin confronts us constantly. Therefore, we're wise when we ask Him to direct our steps so we won't find ourselves tempted to sin against Him. As we go through each day, we face trials that can turn into temptations as we try to maneuver our way around them. Without His leadership in our lives, temptation presents opportunities to nurture our sinful inclinations. At the heart of temptation, **the evil one** can be found. He's always waiting to trap us with His conniving ploys. When we pray, we do well to ask our Father to **deliver** us from the devil's malicious attempts to destroy us by tempting us with choices that wound our relationship with God.

Jesus does not mince His words as He instructs His disciples about another important aspect of forgiveness. When we seek His forgiveness, He forgives us of our sin in keeping with our willingness to **forgive others**. Granted, when we gave our lives to Christ, He forgave us and graced us with the joy of eternal life. Nothing will ever happen to make Him take back His gift of salvation from us. Once He comes into our lives, He never leaves us. Our status before Him as His children will never change. However, unwillingness to forgive others will have a negative effect on the intimacy of our relationship with Him. When we refuse to forgive the **offenses** of others against us, we show a flawed understanding of the forgiveness we have first received. The Greek word for "offence" (*paraptoma*) brings to mind a trespass or deviation from God's way. When we understand the grace we have been shown through Jesus, we will be quick to forgive the trespasses of others against us.

Fasting (6:16-18)

Fasting involves abstaining from food for an extended period of time in order to turn our attention exclusively to the Lord. In the days of the Old Testament, God's people practiced fasting in their walk with the Lord. For example, God's people fasted as they came together in Jerusalem after they returned from exile. As they gathered, they confessed their sins and worshiped Him through the reading of His Word (Nehemiah 9:1-2). Fasting also serves as a personal spiritual discipline. For instance, Daniel fasted as he sought God's forgiveness for Israel who had been taken captive into Babylon (Daniel 9:2-20). During the time of Jesus's ministry, the Pharisees fasted twice each week (Luke 18:12). By using "when" instead of "if" in His instruction, Jesus affirms fasting as an important discipline.

As He teaches His disciples about fasting, He takes a similar approach to His instruction about giving and praying. His chief concern has to do with the need to avoid self-serving hypocrisy and to embrace Christ-centered discipleship. He refers to people who practiced fasting as a means of getting the applause of others as **hypocrites**. Like giving and prayer, fasting became a tool in their quest to play the role of a deeply devoted follower of God. As they acted out the role of an earnest believer, they made themselves look **gloomy** to match the mood of their pretentious efforts to display their fake consecration. Jesus points out that these actors who pretended to have spiritual depth should enjoy the reward they received when others affirmed them. They would receive no **reward** from God for their performance.

YOUR NOTES

As we reflect on the challenge that Jesus gives us, we can appreciate His simple but sobering mandate about fasting. Instead of seeking the accolades of people who watch us, we're wise when we nourish an authentic eagerness to keep our determination to fast to ourselves. The current-day version of Jesus's stern admonition means we will make sure that our hair is clean and combed like always. Likewise, we'll **wash** our faces, take a shower, brush our teeth, put on our clothes, and walk out the door and face the day without giving a clue that we're fasting. What's going on inside us as we engage in our fast will not be **obvious** to those around us. This act of fasting is done in devotion to and worship of the Lord and not as a show for other people.

The journey often turns out to be most rewarding. The spiritual work of cleansing, refocusing, and returning to a life of devotion to our heavenly Father always stands tall as our most precious **reward**. Fasting allows us to know Him better, love Him more, trust Him more completely, and serve Him faithfully. Hope fills our heart as our trust in Him grows stronger through exercising the spiritual discipline of fasting.

We have a number of distractions that prevent us from devoting ourselves to the Lord wholeheartedly and food can often be at the top of the list. No matter the object, we struggle with any number of distractions that keep us from making the Lord our highest priority. Whether it's food or something else, we're wise when we push the distractions away in order to renew our singular devotion to the Lord.

Investing (6:19-21)

As we bring this section of instruction to a close, Jesus introduces another issue that His disciples need to see from His perspective. Underlying His instruction about investing resources is a foundational truth. What we invest in reveals quite a bit about our character. For that reason, Jesus adds investments to the examples He uses to show that what happens to a person on the inside has an effect on what they do on the outside. If a person's heart is turned toward Him, their devotion will be expressed in their investments.

Therefore, disciples with righteous hearts will not give priority to investing in **treasures on earth**. With His directive, Jesus does not intend for people to ignore the need to make wise decisions about financial matters. At the same time, however, He alerts us to the harsh reality that earthly investments run the risk of disappearing at any time. For instance, anyone in Jesus's time who invested in fine clothing ran the risk of having their investment destroyed by a **moth**. Likewise, if someone invested in precious metals, they had to live with the possibility that **rust** may eat away their treasure into nothing of any value. Furthermore, if they placed their hopes in food and put it away in first-century storage units, they may find themselves brokenhearted. One morning, they might open the door to the unit and discover that **thieves** had broken in during the night and stolen all the food they had stored away for the future.

The point that Jesus makes about earthy treasure presents a sobering reality for us today. Like our spiritual siblings in the first century, we cannot rely on our material investments to be trouble-free. Even though we have more safeguards in place, we still have to accept the

YOUR NOTES

fact that we have no guarantees when it comes to our material resources. Changes in stock values and interest rates along with inflation and recession only scratch the surface of the risks we face as we manage our resources in today's financial environment. For that reason, wise believers don't make the accumulation of financial wealth our highest priority.

As Jesus leads us to grow in our walk with Him from the inside out, He directs us to see our wisest choice as we consider our options regarding investments. We choose wisely when we determine that we will favor **treasures in heaven** over those of earth. Jesus reminds us that in making heavenly treasure our priority, we make risk-free investments. Nothing can be taken from us because of a **moth**, a recession, or any other predator when we **store up** heavenly treasures.

Although Jesus directs us to embrace the priority of storing up treasure in heaven, He does not offer specific examples. Along the way, a healthy number of trustworthy leaders in ministry have offered an assortment of helpful suggestions about what counts as heavenly treasure. When we think about what actually gets into heaven from earth, we're left with at least one certainty: people will get there if they have received the gift of salvation through Christ. For that reason, making investments in reaching people with the good news of Christ reaps eternal rewards that can never be taken away. Taking that suggestion seriously means committing resources to such priorities as meeting the needs of others in His name, supporting our local church, and sharing the gospel around the corner and around the world.

Jesus brings His instruction about discipleship back to a believer's **heart**. He reminds us to look into our hearts to see where our **treasure** lies. Taking a look into our hearts could start by answering a simple question: Where do we spend our money? According to Jesus, the answer to that question sheds light on the priorities of your heart.

YOUR NOTES

YOUR NOTES

THE BRIDGE TO WHOLENESS

Jesus instructs us as His disciples to nourish a relationship with Him that starts deep inside the heart. He teaches us about the need to look into our hearts for one important reason—it's the only way we can live out His call to be righteous. Also, it's the only way we can experience authentic spiritual happiness. Jesus guides us to understand being righteous means something different from merely keeping religious rules and rituals. It means nourishing a heart of devotion to Him and reflecting it in the way we treat other people and practice spiritual disciplines (Matthew 5:1–6:21).

As Jesus continues to teach His disciples, He introduces a new word picture. He moves from the heart to the eye. Even though He chose a different word picture, He didn't deviate from the same life principle. With an eye as His word picture, He sets out to teach His disciples the value of seeing the challenges we face from His perspective. Seeing our challenges His way sheds fresh light for us if we open our eyes.

Taking in the Light (6:22-24)

Jesus talked about a healthy **eye** at a time when His listeners lived with the dreadful threat of physical blindness. In those days, birth defects and dangerous infections would take away a person's sight permanently. The people living in Jesus's day knew that no matter how blindness struck someone, it resulted in the same sad outcome. Blindness had no cure. Consequently, Jesus became quite popular because He could make blind people see again. The accounts of His ministry include more than a few episodes in which He healed blind people. For example, He healed two blind men in the Galilean region who asked Him to have mercy of them (Matthew 9:27-31). In Jericho, He healed a blind beggar who sat on the roadside (Mark 10:46-52). In Jerusalem, He restored a man's sight on the Sabbath, which landed Him and the man He healed into trouble with the Pharisees (John 9:1-7).

Spiritual vision mattered to Jesus too. His concern prompted Him to challenge the Pharisees by calling them blind guides who led others to suffer from the same spiritual blindness (Matthew 15:10-14). Although their blindness made them reject Him as Messiah, they considered themselves to have clear spiritual eyesight.

The sensitivity of Jesus to the malady of blindness and the need for people to be able to see served as the setting for His instruction about the eye. He uses the reality of physical eyesight to impress upon His disciples the value of being able to see well spiritually. In doing so, He notes an accepted principle regarding eyesight. The eye serves as a **lamp** that allows light to come into a person's **body**. Jesus used light as an illustration earlier in His instruction when He declared that His followers were the light of the world (5:14). Now Jesus brings up another well-known feature of light to teach an important spiritual insight. Being **full of light** would keep a person's body **healthy**. In the same way, nourishing healthy spiritual eyesight would allow His disciples to grow in their walk with Him. His instruction resonated with the Old Testament testimony that God's Word served as a light for His people (Psalm 119:105; Proverbs 6:23).

YOUR NOTES

Physical light streaming into a person's body from the sunshine or a lamp provided Jesus with a picture that encouraged His listeners to maintain healthy spiritual eyesight. Nobody had to tell them about what happened when an **eye** went **bad**. The light couldn't get into the **body**, which would leave a person disabled. Although the body needed light in order to go in the right direction, a bad eye would keep it **full of darkness**. Consequently, anyone with a bad eye would not have the light necessary to take the right path. As Jesus said, a person struck with complete blindness lived in total **darkness**. By the same token, someone disabled by spiritual **darkness** would be completely blind to the Lord's direction. No one would ever choose to live in such **deep** darkness. Therefore, followers of Jesus seek to maintain healthy spiritual eyesight so they can allow the light of His presence, power, wisdom, and love to fill their lives completely.

We do well to reflect seriously on the instruction of Jesus. He's the Light of the world, and He promises us that we'll never walk in darkness because He'll provide us with "the light of life" (John 8:12).

Jesus allows His light to shine into the lives of His disciples as He brings into view the issue of ultimate control. As He presents His perspective on who or what got the final word in their lives, He mentions **masters**. His disciples living then would have been familiar with the meaning of the title. Slavery existed in Israel long before the ministry of Jesus. Old Testament passages like Exodus 21:1-21, Leviticus 25:39-55, and Deuteronomy 15:12-18 provided God's people with laws to be obeyed and principles to be respected by masters and slaves. Slavery continued into and beyond the days of Jesus and His ministry. In New Testament passages like Ephesians 6:5-8, Colossians 3:22-25, Philemon 8-16, and 1 Peter 2:18-21, the apostles directed believers in the churches regarding masters and slaves. Incidentally, Romans 1:1, James, 1:1, and 2 Peter 1:1 used terms from the realm of slavery to describe absolute devotion to Jesus.

The orientation of the disciples to masters and slaves would have made them aware of the truth that He shared with them about ultimate control. A slave would never be able to **serve** with wholehearted devotion **two** different masters at the same time. Such a possibility would never have existed. Eventually one of the masters would have complete control over the slave.

As we apply the teaching of Jesus to our culture, we cannot make the comparison that serving two masters in the days of Jesus would be like having two employers today. Even with two different employers, most employees enjoy a certain level of liberty. In some cases, laws protect their liberties. For instance, they're able to bring their work to a close at the end of the day or night. They also have the freedom to choose how they spend the time away from their jobs. In addition, they have the liberty to change their employers.

First-century slaves had no such liberty. In fact, they had no freedom at all. Therefore, they could not choose how they would live, what they would do, or how long they would have to work. They belonged to masters who always had the final word in every aspect of their lives.

Jesus points out that serving two masters is not possible because the affections of the slaves would draw them to one master and away from the other. Eventually, one master would be hated, and the other master would be loved. The love for one of the masters would

YOUR NOTES

give way to complete **devotion**, while the other master would be **despised**.

Having introduced an impossibility that would have made sense to His listeners, Jesus applies it to a pressing spiritual issue. He points His disciples to the impossibility of thinking they can **serve God and money** at the same time. His perspective sheds helpful light on decisions about loyalties. With healthy spiritual insight, they would be able to see His perspective and embrace it.

So can disciples today if our eyes remain open to the truth about divided loyalties. The Greek word for money (*mamonas*) conveys the general idea of personal wealth. Either disciples of Jesus will devote themselves fully to Him, or we will be obsessed with gathering up more wealth for ourselves. If we enslave ourselves to the quest for more wealth, we will love money with unbending loyalty. In turn, we will eventually turn our backs on the Lord. We'll find ourselves resenting His constant nudges about the need to be loyal to Him. However, if we devote ourselves to the Lord as our highest priority, we will take hold of the perspective of Jesus about our wealth. We'll see it as a resource that we can use so we will serve Him well. Such a Christ-centered perspective is shaped by the light of Christ as we allow Him to fill our lives.

The instruction of Jesus about our loyalties cannot be overlooked. If we open our eyes to it so we can put it to work, we will exhibit that we have good eyes and that we want to take in His light so we will not stumble in the darkness of other perspectives.

Doing Away with Worry (6:25-30)

A natural question arises from a disciple's determination to devote him or herself to Jesus instead of money. How will we pay our everyday expenses? If we put the question in the context of the first-century disciples, our concern would swirl around getting enough **food** and **clothing**. The question points to a pressing life issue for believers in any time frame. Complete devotion to Jesus can bring on **worry** about the basic necessities of **life**.

Jesus sheds light on the concern by giving us His perspective. If we take it in, it will enlighten us so we see clearly. In turn, we'll give up worrying constantly about our needs when we learn how to keep trusting Him. He brings His perspective into view with a key transition word—**therefore**. Jesus's teaching on God's provision comes on the heels of His insistence that we serve Him alone and not our money. With the transition word, He **tells** us about some of the practical ways that we put our complete devotion to Him into everyday practice. To begin with, we can set aside our tendency to worry about what we need as we serve Him. Notice that He talks about worry and anxiety quite often as He instructs us about living out our devotion to Him, and for good reason. We can get worried about what we need in **life**. Our list of worries includes what we will **eat** or **drink** or what we will have on hand to **wear**. Jesus responds by reminding us that living well involves much more than food and clothing. Therefore, if having enough **food** or **clothing** abides as our chief concern, we're overlooking what really brings lasting fulfillment in life. Nothing other than a personal relationship with Him as a growing disciple makes our lives worth living. Of course, food and clothing have a place in our relationship with Him. For that reason, we can trust Him to

YOUR NOTES

see to it that we have everything we need.

As Jesus addresses the problem of fretting over food, He turns to a **sky** full of **birds** that appeared to be perfectly content. The obvious contentment of the birds stands out more prominently when Jesus mentions the precarious nature of their existence. He notes that they make no effort whatsoever to supply themselves with food. Every day they fly high above the heads of farmers who spend every working day in their fields. The farmer's agricultural labor consists of preparing the ground, sowing the seeds, reaping the harvest, and gathering the crops to be stored in **barns**. The backbreaking work of a farmer never ends. In stark contrast, the birds never come close to this labor-intensive procedure for producing food. Yet, they are fed well enough to fly, sing, perch, and nest whenever they please.

How did the birds keep from fretting over their next meal? Jesus gives His disciples the answer to the question. Their **heavenly Father** feeds them. At the right time and in His perfect way, He provides them with what they need to eat. Jesus goes further to proclaim that their Father in heaven loves people much more than birds. He created birds simply by using His voice and "speaking" them into existence (Genesis 1:20-23). When He created Adam, however, He used His own hands to form him and breathed life into him (Genesis 2:7). Likewise, He created Eve with His own hands by taking a rib from Adam and using it as He formed her (Genesis 2:20-22). His intimacy in bringing Adam and Eve to life underscored the value that He placed on people. Because they are **worth more** to Him, His people can count on Him to be faithful to take care of them.

Before Jesus moves on with His instruction, He brings up a pearl of wisdom that continues to settle worried followers of Christ. **Worrying** does not produce anything that will help us as we serve Him. Worry won't add **one moment** to our lives. Wise believers know that fretting is like sitting in a rocking chair. Rocking back and forth in it gives us something to do, but it doesn't get us anywhere.

Next, Jesus sheds light on the habit of becoming anxious about **clothes**. In those days, everyday clothes included basic garments like a loincloth, a tunic, a cloak, a belt, and sandals. People wore clothes for the sake of modesty, but also as protection from the harsh climate. For instance, if they didn't have a cloak, they would expose themselves to the danger of extreme heat and sunlight during the day or the drastic changes in temperature during the night. Therefore, not having proper clothing stood out as a valid reason for being anxious.

Jesus responds to the worry over being clothed by pointing to **wildflowers** that grow in the **field**. They clothed the landscapes of Israel with incomparable beauty, and they appeared to do it effortlessly. In those days, making clothes started with the hard work of producing cloth. The material for the cloth had to be spun into threads either by hand or with spinning tools. In turn, the threads had to be woven into a piece of fabric. Nobody ever saw the wildflowers put any **labor** into their breathtaking displays of color that covered the fields. Jesus says that their displays outshine the **splendor** of King Solomon's unforgettable building and expansion projects. Of course, the magnificent temple in Jerusalem stood tall as his most impressive architectural accomplishment (1 Kings 5–8). Even the superlative beauty of Solomon's signature construction project pales in comparison to the unequaled adornment of the fields that the wildflowers render.

One important detail about the wildflowers and their incredible displays deserves sincere consideration. The flowers burst forth with beautiful colors, but not for long. Wildflowers

YOUR NOTES

have a short life-span. Jesus reminds us that they are **here today**, but they are gathered up and thrown into a furnace to be burned **tomorrow**. They're burned in the furnace because they've withered and died after living for only a little while. Even though they don't last long, God makes sure that they return with new growth at just the right time. We can rest assured that He cares for us even more, and He will **do much more** for us.

The anxiety over whether we'll be supplied with what we need as we serve the Lord has nothing to do with His lack of faithfulness. As Jesus points out, a sincere look at the wild birds and wildflowers should convince us that we can count on Him to give us everything necessary. Our worry has everything to do with our lack of **faith** in Him.

Jesus exposes the lack of faith that threatens His disciples. In this portion of His instruction, He brought to light their need to be honest with themselves about how much they trusted Him. His statement about the **little faith** that existed in them served as candid rebuke. At the same time, it provided them with the opportunity to open their eyes so they could let the light of His perspective into their lives. The more they took in the spiritual light that He shared, the better they could see that they should take the path of faith in Him.

Throughout His ministry, Jesus had to return to the issue of weak faith quite often as He led His disciples. Matthew recorded some of the episodes in which Jesus held His disciples accountable for their lack of faith in Him. For instance, their fear of a storm revealed the weakness of their faith (Matthew 8:26). Later, He rescued Peter from sinking into the water on which he had previously walked and underscored the lack of faith in His disciples (Matthew 14:31). On another occasion, when He heard His disciples fretting over not having enough bread, He told them it was a lack of faith that prompted their anxiety (Matthew 16:7-8).

Seeking God's Kingdom (6:31-34)

Disciples today struggle with faith too. We're like the first-century followers of Christ in that our faith needs to be strengthened. Like the disciples then, we tend to ask Jesus to "increase our faith" (Luke 17:5). With such a request, we give the impression that faith is like water in a pitcher that Jesus can pour into us. Growing disciples learn that faith is more like a muscle that's stretched and strengthened every time it's used.

Jesus tells us that when we turn to Him by faith, we do well to take an approach that's completely different from the path taken by those who don't know Him personally. They **worry** about their unmet needs. Jesus listed some of the unmet needs that usually cause them to be anxious. They don't have enough to **eat** or **drink**, and they don't have adequate clothing. Their worry may lead them to pray, but their prayer consists solely of delivering their list of needs. According to Jesus, the **Gentiles** used such an approach as they appealed to their pagan deities for help with the needs that caused them to fret. Their eagerness to have their needs met prompted them to appeal to their idols. Their hearts were set on having their needs met, not nourishing a relationship with a deity. They kept on pursuing their deities in order to solicit divine attention. They thought that their needs would not be addressed if they failed to compel the deities to notice them. The lack of uncertainty about getting noticed by the idol led them to fret even more. Therefore, the more they prayed, the more they fretted.

YOUR NOTES

For growing followers of the Lord, time in prayer has an altogether different outcome, made possible through faith in God. Instead of pestering a divine dispenser that won't be available to help, disciples of Jesus find contentment in turning to our **heavenly Father**. We know that He loves us because He demonstrates it in countless ways. Of course, the superlative evidence is Jesus. We don't live in the worry that He's not available, He won't understand, or He doesn't care about us. On the contrary, we're satisfied in the certainty that He knows us intimately, and He cares about us constantly. Our heavenly Father never loses sight of us, and He wants us to grow deeper in our personal relationship with Him. That's why He sent Jesus to be our Savior. When we receive His gift of salvation, the door to a lasting personal walk with our heavenly Father opens for eternity.

In light of the faithfulness of our heavenly Father, we take seriously the instruction that Jesus gives about getting rid of worry. We have the only reliable way to put our anxiety behind us. He knows that turning to Him with our eyes focused exclusively on our need will not work. We will only become more anxious. However, when we turn to Him with an eagerness to **seek** Him through a true and lasting relationship, we can expect a different outcome. We'll see for ourselves that He's able to work in us to set aside our anxiety. As we follow Him, we learn to trust Him and His faithfulness. As we abide in the assurance of His faithfulness, our faith in Him grows stronger and more enduring.

Jesus asserts that growing in an intimate relationship with Him means seeking His **kingdom** instead of seeking a temporary relief for our anxiety. What's involved in seeking His kingdom? It does not involve working hard or staying busy so we'll earn our keep as kingdom citizens. Rather, it encompasses what Jesus has already taught us so far about being His disciples. Seeking His kingdom means taking hold of what makes us authentically happy as we grow spiritually in Him. It also means being salt and light by having a **righteousness** in Him that grows inside our hearts and shows up in our words and actions. Accordingly, we don't let anger overwhelm us, we don't treat others as objects to be tossed aside when we're finished with them, and we are forbearing because we love others like He loves us. Also, we allow the light of His presence to fill us so we can see clearly how to give, pray, and fast in ways that reflect His light in our lives. As we seek His kingdom, worry doesn't hamper us because our faith in Him strengthens us. Equally important, we can live in the certainty that everything we need as we serve Him will **be provided** because of His faithfulness.

The apostle Paul testified that seeking the kingdom of God would drive away worry and prompt us to grow in faith. In his letter to the Philippian church, he noted that he had learned how to be content. His contentment had nothing to do with having plenty or living in poverty. He came to see that His contentment came from being with Jesus. As a result, he found that he could do anything because Jesus strengthened him (Philippians 4:11-13). Paul's testimony underscores the value of the instruction that Jesus gives about seeking His kingdom and His righteousness as our first priority. When we follow His instruction, worry over our needs will diminish as our faith in Him grows more durable.

Of course, the assurance Jesus gives has to be understood in the context of eternity. We know that we can count on Him to be faithful to us. He will provide us with what we need. His provision may come in this life or in the age to come. Either way, we trust Him completely to know and do what's best for us. Therefore, seasoned believers do not fret over

YOUR NOTES

troubling challenges. As an example, the bad news that comes from medical procedures may shock us, but it won't leave us paralyzed. Our trust in Him keeps us steady as we face uncertainties that come our way.

As Jesus finishes this portion of His instruction about having good spiritual vision in order to take in His light, He gives His disciples then and now an assignment. He introduces it with the same signpost word He used before—**therefore**. Based on what He has taught us so far, we're assigned the task of not worrying **about tomorrow**. Refusing to fret about the future does not mean we have His permission to be irresponsible. Neither does it imply that we can fool ourselves into thinking we can be lazy with our time. Growing as a disciple includes taking seriously the call to carry out His work (John 9:4).

Jesus's instruction about tomorrow takes us back to a thought-provoking portion of His model prayer. In the prayer, He challenges us to turn to our heavenly Father daily and ask Him to provide us with what we'll need for the day (Matthew 6:11). We're wise when we trust Him to help us each day. Conversely, we're foolish if we fret over the uncertainties of the future.

Worrying about tomorrow robs us of the contentment He wants us to enjoy today. Besides, worrying about the future won't change it. Jesus assures us that **each day** will bring **trouble** with it. The Greek word for "trouble" (*kakia*) denotes wickedness or affliction. While the possibility of trouble awaiting us tomorrow may be unsettling, the reality of our heavenly Father's presence in the future encourages us. We can trust Him to be there and to provide us with what we'll need. For that reason, His disciples learn to leave the future in His hands. We do our best when we focus our attention on today and how He intends for us to deal with the challenges facing us now.

YOUR NOTES

YOUR NOTES

YOUR NOTES

THE RIGHT WAY TO JUDGE

Thanks to the instruction that Jesus has given, mature disciples understand the value of nurturing spiritual eyesight and the best way to put it to work as we walk with Him. Healthy spiritual eyesight allows the light of His presence to shine brightly into our lives. In turn, we're able to see ourselves and others from His perspective. With His insights, we're able to make wise choices regarding loyalty. Instead of being obsessed with money, for example, we devote ourselves wholeheartedly to Him. Also, healthy spiritual eyesight provides us with relief from anxiety as we make the kingdom of God our first priority.

With keen eyes open to the perspective of Jesus, we can also make sensible judgments. As Jesus continues to guide us so we can grow well spiritually, He challenges us to work from the inside out as we strengthen our relationships with others and with Him. The effect of choosing such a spiritually mature path can be seen in our determination to practice spiritual discernment. As discerning disciples, we will make the best judgments regarding people. We will also be wise regarding our eagerness to share the good news of Christ. In addition, we will trust God to be faithful when we ask Him for help.

Judging Others (7:1-5)

As we take a look into the issue of judging others, our first instinct as disciples of Jesus may be to declare that we're in no position to **judge** anyone. We affirm that only the Lord has the authority and wisdom for rendering appropriate judgment. His authority to judge perfectly comes from His work in creation, His character of holiness, His eternal sovereignty, His unequaled wisdom, and His consistent compassion. He expresses these and other attributes in keeping with His redemptive plan that centers in Jesus. Therefore, loyal believers honor Him and give Him all the glory. He alone sits on the throne of His kingdom as the matchless Lord who judges everyone everywhere. Nobody can escape His judgment (Psalm 75:7; 96:13; Ecclesiastes 3:17; Romans 2:3).

Growing believers affirm that only God possesses the qualifications to serve as our eternal judge. At the same time, we acknowledge that we find ourselves quite often in situations that require us to make judgments about the people in our world. The Greek word for "judge" (*krino*) carries the idea of evaluating for the sake of coming to a decision. Every day we have to evaluate individuals so we can make prudent decisions about them. For example, we have to engage in evaluation so we can make decisions about the neighbors next door, the doctor who takes care of us when we're sick, the banker who handles our money, the political leader who wants our vote, and the person who makes a delivery to our front door. Our decision comes on the heels of our evaluation of the folks who step in and out of our lives. We evaluate everything from their skills to their motives to their integrity.

Of course, as we make judgments about others, we're hampered by the hard reality that we base our decisions solely on what we can know with regard to their words and actions. We can't look into their hearts. Granted, we're able to see the evidence of what's in their

YOUR NOTES

hearts a little more as we get to know them better. But even in our best moments, we can't see their hearts completely. Only the Lord knows what's going on in the hearts of people who come in and out of our lives (Psalm 44:21; Acts 15:8).

The Lord reminds us of our limitations when it comes to judging others. We know that we can't see in others what He can clearly see in them. For that reason, growing disciples avoid judging people until we have walked around in their shoes for a while. Accommodating ourselves to these limitations can prevent us from embracing one of two extremes when it comes to judging others. Either we pledge that we will wash our hands of the responsibility of judging another person, or we will grow a little too fond of occupying the throne of judgment. If we take an extreme measure and decide that we will not ever judge anyone, we set ourselves up for disappointment. We'll disappoint ourselves when threatening situations force us to make a judgment about an individual or group as a matter of safety or security. Our frustration over having to make judgments about others can leave us with a heavy load of unrelenting guilt and shame that we carry around in our hearts.

However, the other extreme can be far more damaging. This extreme has to do with the satisfaction we get when we empower ourselves with the role of judging others. If we begin to enjoy the power rush that comes with being judges, we'll run the risk of becoming heartless and cruel as we cast a judgmental or prejudicial gaze on people. When we empower ourselves in this way, we make judgments about them too easily without even knowing them. By the time we give in to this extreme pattern, we've made prefabricated decisions about people based on what they look like, how they talk, who they associate with, or what they wear.

The tension between both extremes can be most difficult for us to manage. How can we judge others in a way that reflects our sincere loyalty to Jesus? We can be grateful that Jesus addresses the question and provides us with the best answer. He points us to the **standard** to keep in view when we find ourselves having to make judgments about others. He reminds us that the **same** standard will be used when it's our turn to be judged.

The disciples of Jesus must have been grateful that He did not leave them in the dark with His answer. As He elaborates, He incorporates a word picture that He used previously. When He taught His disciples about how to deal with the challenges associated with their loyalty to Him, He told them about the need to have a good eye—spiritually speaking—so they could see His perspective, be enlightened by it, and embrace it (Matthew 6:22-34). Now He points His disciples to a problem related to poor spiritual eyesight. He shows them the tendency to notice the **splinter** in their **brother's eye** while at the same time ignoring the **beam of wood** lodged in their **own** eyes. After pointing to the problem, He asks His disciples **why** they would be able to pass judgment on their spiritual siblings while they remain spiritually blind to the monumental issues that block their vision about themselves.

Jesus doesn't stop there. He raises a follow-up question for His disciples. He ask them to tell Him **how** such blind believers can assert themselves as role models of spirituality. While they affirm their superior ability to correct the spiritual vision problems of other believers, they ignore their own blindness that disables them to the point that they can't see at all. They identify themselves as the source of sound judgment for others who have made errors in their walk with the Lord. At the same time, they disregard the obvious need to take a

YOUR NOTES

long look in the mirror. For that reason, Jesus calls them **hypocrites** who parade their false piety for everyone to admire. They deceive others and perhaps themselves into thinking that they possess the necessary spiritual depth required to make sound judgments about people. In order to correct their blindness, they have to see themselves as Jesus sees them. As they do, their blindness will be replaced with clarity of vision. In turn, they are able to make sound judgments and speaks words of life to other believers with integrity and humility.

With discerning eyes, we take the time necessary to evaluate the areas of our lives from which "beam of wood" tendencies may be hiding. Asking the Lord to help us to take an honest look into our hearts can prevent us from going spiritually blind. In His presence, we always have healthy opportunities to evaluate our spiritual eyesight.

Sharing the Gospel (7:6)

As Jesus continues, He introduces another area in which spiritual discernment is required. He instructs them to be discerning as they reach out to others around them. The principle He shares may have been jolting to His disciples, at least at first. Once more, His masterful use of word pictures conveys the serious warning so they can comprehend it more completely.

The Jewish followers of Jesus had the Old Testament Scripture affirming God's holiness (1 Samuel 2:2; Psalm 77:13; 99:9). The Scripture also affirmed the need for His people to be holy (Leviticus 11:44; 19:2; 20:7). Being **holy** meant being set apart. Therefore, God was set apart entirely by Himself, and His people were set apart to serve Him exclusively. When Jesus warns His followers not to **give** what is holy **to dogs**, He brings into view whatever has been set apart for God and used according to His purpose. Generations of notable Bible students have offered insightful suggestions as to what Jesus may have been referring to when He mentioned what was holy. For believers on the other side of the cross, the gospel of Christ is holy. From the outset of the ministry of Jesus, He proclaimed the gospel (Mark 1:14). After His resurrection, He commissioned His disciples to keep on sharing the gospel everywhere (Matthew 28:18-20; Luke 24:46-48). The good news of Christ has been set apart for God's eternal purpose of providing the gift of salvation.

The disciples heard Jesus say that He did not want them to share what was holy with **dogs**. He did not use the Greek word for tamed dogs that enjoyed the privilege of being house pets. Instead, He used a word that brought to mind vicious mongrels that ran wild throughout the region and wreaked havoc on livestock and people alike. Accordingly, Jewish people used the word to refer to Gentiles. Jesus brings up dogs as He talks about the way that some people would respond to the gospel. They would get close enough to the good news of Jesus to take a look at it. When they concluded that it would fail to satisfy their pagan appetites, they would reject it. Their rejection would be marked by extreme anger that would prompt them to respond with hateful animosity for the good news of Christ as well as anyone who shared it with them.

Jesus goes on to share another set of alarming word pictures. He warns His disciples about tossing their **pearls before pigs**. The people living in the days of the New Testament

YOUR NOTES

appreciated the value of pearls. Jesus compares the kingdom of God to a pearl in a parable about a man who sold everything he had so he could buy a field that had a priceless pearl buried in it (Matthew 13:44-46). In John's vision of new Jerusalem, pearls served as gates to the city (Revelation 21:21). In stark contrast, pigs represented the most disgusting animal of all. Jewish people detested pigs because they were considered unclean. For that reason, they referred to Gentiles as pigs. A pig would never be a house pet or an animal kept in a pen on a Jewish farm. In those days, pigs were wild, and they were dangerous. Like dogs, they were driven by their ravenous appetites. Therefore, if anyone tossed a priceless pearl in front of a famished pig, trouble would certainly follow. The pig would see the pearl as a morsel to be eaten. Therefore, it would become enraged when its food turned out to be anything but edible. Animosity would grow out of the disappointment that the pearl did not satisfy the pig's gnawing hunger. Disappointment could give way to violence, leading the pig to trample the pearl into the ground on its way to attacking the person who tossed it. Pigs were known for their savagery. They would **tear** their victims **to pieces** when they attacked them.

Of course, the Jewish leaders fit the description of the dogs and pigs that Jesus described. Throughout His ministry, He preached the gospel. He proclaimed the truth about repentance and faith as He declared that kingdom of God had "come near" (Mark 1:14-15). The resentment of the Jewish leaders at the beginning of His ministry turned into enraged hatred for Him. In turn, they attacked Him at every turn in their relentless effort to do away with Him.

As we share the good news of salvation through Jesus, we're wise when we take the instruction of Jesus seriously. We need to be discerning enough to make wise judgments about when to present the good news and how it should be presented.

Trusting God (7:7-8)

So far, Jesus has directed us to be discerning about the judgments we make. We'll be accountable for how we judge people in our lives. Also, He has warned us to use discretion as we share the gospel with others. Many will reject of the good news of salvation through Christ and may unleash their hostility toward God on His disciples (Colossians 1:21).

As He continues to teach us about practicing discernment when we make judgments, He turns to our relationship with God and how we approach Him with our needs. He directs us to be persistent when we pray. When we practice persistence, we testify that we trust Him to hear and answer us when we share our concerns with Him. Our persistence can take the form of asking, or it could be more like seeking. It may even take the shape of knocking. We also reflect our persistence in the way that we "keep on praying" and "keep on seeking" and "keep on knocking" (NLT). Of course, persistence in prayer for a follower of Christ looks completely different from the empty babbling of pagans as they try to get the attention of their idols (Matthew 6:7).

We can count on Him to respond to us. Likewise, we trust Him to respond in keeping with His wisdom regarding what's best for us. For that reason, we turn to Him and **ask** for what we need. He will respond by giving what He knows we need in His time and in His way.

YOUR NOTES

Similarly, when our praying looks more like seeking, we can rest in the assurance that our search will not be in vain. He will guide us so we will **find** what we're searching for, and He will do so in perfect alignment with His plan for us.

The same assurance comes our way when we find ourselves praying in a way that bears a striking resemblance to knocking on a door. With the word picture in mind, we see ourselves standing on the outside of a house or outside a room with the door closed in front of us. By knocking on the door, we're asking for access. Using this same word picture, Jesus later presents Himself standing outside the church of Laodicea and knocking on the door. Opening the door removes the obstacle that's been keeping Him outside. When the door is opened and He steps inside, fellowship commences (Revelation 3:20). When our prayer takes the shape of knocking on the door to Him, we can be certain that **it will be opened** and He will open the door in keeping with what's best for us.

When we take Jesus at His word that He will respond, we'll keep on praying. We'll decide to persist in prayer until He responds. When we view our request through His eyes, we may realize that it's really not what we need after all. Persistent prayer enables us to gain a sharper perspective on what we actually need. In turn, we won't miss His response to our prayer because we've been looking for a different answer. Of course, He may delay in His response while He's leading us to see something we need to address with Him, ourselves, or others. For instance, He may be waiting for us to forgive someone before He opens the door to deeper intimacy with Him.

The issue with persistence in prayer has nothing to do with God's faithfulness. The issue has everything to do with our willingness to persist. If we lack discernment, we will run the risk of making a foolish judgment about God and His faithfulness. When He delays in response, we may decide foolishly to give up on Him. However, wise judgment takes us in a different direction in our walk with Him. Guided by wisdom, we'll practice discernment, and we'll keep on praying in faith that He will respond. We live in the confidence that even though He's silent, He's not absent.

Incidentally, Jesus elsewhere shared two parables that underscored the value of persistent prayer. In Luke 11:5-10, Jesus told the parable of three friends. In the parable, He underscored His directive for His disciples to devote themselves to diligence in prayer by asking, seeking, and knocking. This parable includes one friend who went to his friend with the request for three loaves of bread for another friend. His friend to whom he made his request did not share any loaves of bread with him, at least at first. In due time, however, he gave his friend as much bread as he needed. With the parable, Jesus reinforced the importance of persistence in prayer.

In Luke 18:1-8, Jesus shared another parable about not giving up on prayer. In the parable, a powerless widow appealed to an uncaring judge for justice. Because she had no political power, the judge ignored her plea. But his silence did not prevent her from returning to him repeatedly with the same request. Eventually, the judge gave in to her constant appeals and granted her request for judgment.

With these parables, Jesus helps us see that He understands the temptation to give up on prayer. Our frustration may give way to judging that God won't respond. Instead of giving in to the temptation and growing frustrated or disillusioned, we're wise when we keep trusting Him and keep praying in the certainty that He hears us. We can count on His faithfulness.

Seeking the Kingdom (7:9-12)

YOUR NOTES

Jesus takes the issue of faithfulness one step further by referencing a father's relationship with his children. In an everyday setting that His disciples could appreciate, He describes a son who would go to his father and ask him for a piece of **bread**. In those days, bread was a basic item in a family's diet. Therefore, a **son's** request to his father for bread would not have been out of the ordinary. The request represented the child's awareness that his father supplied him with what he needed. Having provided the ordinary picture of an everyday occurrence, Jesus moves on to ask a question that may have been a little shocking to His disciples. Would the boy's father give him a **stone** instead of bread? Of course, the answer was obvious. The boy's dad would not do something so ridiculous. A stone could not be eaten. Accordingly, it would have been nothing less than a cruel insult to a hungry child. Furthermore, it would have shown that the boy's dad had no interest whatsoever in meeting his son's need for something to eat.

Next, Jesus introduces another everyday request that children would make to their parents. Instead of bread, this time the little boy asked his father for a **fish**, another staple item in a family's meal at that time. The fish would have been nutritious, and it would have been available. Would the boy expect his dad to give him a **snake** instead of a fish? Of course not. A fish would have fed the little boy, but a snake would have bitten him. Once more, such a response to a child's request would have been an insult to his need for food as well as a threat to his life.

What the boy asked his dad to give him would have been good for him. Both of the items he requested would have helped him. In response, his dad would not give him something that would have hurt him. He would not be inclined to turn his son's requests into opportunities to play heartless pranks on him.

Guiding us on the path toward grasping the extent of God's faithfulness, Jesus shows us the only logical conclusion that can be drawn about trusting Him. He starts by acknowledging that people are **evil** according to their flesh. With their words and actions, they display the brokenness of their lives. They can exhibit this in plenty of ways. Still, even though parents are susceptible to evil because they're sinners, they exhibit positive traits with their **children**. Most parents, even those far from God, will do everything possible to help their kids to grow up in a healthy environment. The thought of playing cruel jokes on their children would never cross their minds. In fact, they would make any sacrifice necessary in order to provide **good gifts** for them.

Making His point using a comparison of lesser to greater, Jesus invites us to compare the treatment of caring parents for their children with God's care for us. We belong to Him as His children, and He is our **Father in heaven**. Earthly parents have evil in their nature. Evil doesn't exist in God's heart. Therefore, the notion that He would mistreat His children is impossible. Therefore, we can always depend on Him to be faithful to **give** us **good things**. When we turn to Him and present our needs, we can rest assured that He will respond with what's best for us.

We may not always agree with Him or His response to our request. Initially, we may be tempted to make the opposite judgment about Him. We may ponder the notion that

YOUR NOTES

He's thoughtless, uncaring, or downright cruel. In due time, however, we will see that He provides us with what's best for us. For that reason, we're wise when we trust Him even over our present experience. Wise disciples agree with Paul's assertion that the Lord is faithful (1 Thessalonians 5:24).

Jesus summarized His instruction about the need for discernment in judging others, sharing the gospel, and trusting God's faithfulness with a principle that has come to be known as the Golden Rule. As we serve Him, we demonstrate wisdom by doing for others as we would like them **to do for us**. Living out this principle requires us to be discerning when we make judgments regarding our relationships with ourselves, and others in our world. In Matthew 22:40, the link between the Great Commandment and the totality of God's Word is underscored. Similarly, the so-called Golden Rule is marked by the same connection with **the Law and the Prophets**. When we live according to the golden rule, we display God the Father's heart to others.

YOUR NOTES

YOUR NOTES

TWO WAYS OF LIVING

In the Sermon on the Mount, Jesus guided His disciples to embrace His way to authentic happiness, and He underscored His work of fulfilling the law instead of getting rid of it. He taught His disciples they were to live as salt and light in the world as He directed them to nourish true righteousness from the inside out. He taught them that righteousness from their hearts would be evident in their relationships with others as well as in their attention to spiritual disciplines, spiritual eyesight, and spiritual discernment.

Before He finished this sermon, He told His disciples what they would need to do with His instruction. He intended for them to put the insights they had gained to work in their lives in order to serve Him well. In turn, the desire to serve Him well would nurture their ongoing commitment to discipleship. Along these lines, Jesus finished His sermon by summarizing His teaching by laying out multiple important decisions. He couched the decisions in terms of two gates, two trees, and two foundations.

Two Gates (7:13-14)

Having taught His disciples how to grow toward spiritual fulfillment in Him, Jesus presents them with a choice about how to embrace what He taught them. He described the choice for His disciples in terms of two gates that led to two extremely different roads.

Growing believers of any generation can comprehend discipleship as a lifelong journey in which we follow Jesus every step of the way. And like any other journey, the determination to follow Jesus has a starting place. Jesus points to the beginning of the journey by referring to a **gate**. He goes even further to direct us so we can see which gate we must **enter** to follow Him on the journey of discipleship. For believers, entering the narrow gate serves as a way to think about receiving the gift of salvation through Him. When we give our lives to Him, we begin the journey of discipleship as born-again spiritual infants (John 3:3). But we aren't to remain satisfied with spiritual infancy. Instead, we devote ourselves to growing spiritually toward maturity as we walk in His steps daily.

The disciples who listened as Jesus described the beginning of the journey heard Him say that He wanted them to enter the **narrow** gate. He had more to say about the narrow gate, but first He contrasted it with the **gate** He described as **wide**. Those who enter the wide gate place themselves on a **broad road**.

The options Jesus presents include only two gates, and each option has serious consequences. People live out their choice by taking the road awaiting them on the other side of the gate they select. Accordingly, the wide gate would lead to a road that's broad. Jesus notes that **many** people would choose to go **through** the wide gate that would put them on the broad road; it is the popular choice.

Once we receive the gift of salvation, we begin a lifelong journey that's meant to take us from spiritual infancy to maturity. To not make a decision about the gates is to make a decision. If we do nothing with the claims of Jesus, we'll find ourselves entering through the wide gate because it requires no effort and is the path of least resistance. Because the gate

YOUR NOTES

is so wide, we can take all of the baggage that we want along with us on our journey. Those who enter by the wide gate decide—directly or indirectly—that what Jesus teaches us about being authentically happy doesn't really interest us.

Even though the wide gate looks attractive, choosing it would be foolish. Jesus warns His disciples that walking through the wide gate and taking the broad road leads **to destruction**. The Greek word for destruction (*apollumi*) brings to mind the reality of being utterly ruined or suffering extreme loss. It points to the awful outcome of spiritual destitution that awaits those who choose the broad road.

With the crushing consequence associated with taking the wide gate and the broad road as the backdrop, Jesus returns to the narrow gate. Incidentally, when Jesus mentioned the narrow gate the first time, He used a Greek word (*stenos*) that indicates a path that would be the opposite of what people would prefer. When He uses the word "narrow" the second time, He uses another Greek word (*thlibo*). It portrays a demanding and punishing mountain path that would crush anyone who tried to take it alone. The word implies the road that persecuted believers would travel because of their loyalty to Him. Choosing to go through such a narrow gate means facing the difficulties associated with embracing authentic happiness, being salt and light, and exhibiting righteousness that grows from a transformed heart. This is reflected in the way His disciples treat others, embrace spiritual disciplines, express their loyalty, and seek spiritual discernment. Undoubtedly, choosing the narrow gate leads to a **difficult** road. Even so, the choice is worth it because it leads to **life**.

With the picture that Jesus offers us about the narrow gate and the difficult road, He does not imply that His disciples must do something to earn eternal life. Quite the opposite, eternal life is a gift we receive freely. With His assurance about life that comes when we walk through the narrow gate of discipleship, He brings into view the spiritual fulfillment that we enjoy here on earth and later in heaven. Even when following resembles taking a rugged and demanding path in which we meet persecution because we belong to Him, we find true happiness with the journey. And even though others decide not to embrace the demands of discipleship, those who do will have no regrets. We can be settled in the reality that the best way of living is found in following Him wherever He leads us.

Two Trees (7:15-23)

As we follow Jesus on the journey of discipleship, we'll have company along the way. We'll be joined by our spiritual brothers and sisters who share life in Christ together with us. However, Jesus warns to expect others to join us whose company we would be wise not to keep. Staying on **guard** enables us to keep from being hoodwinked by false prophets who accompany us with the intention of deceiving us.

In the Old Testament, God promised His people that He would bring prophets to them who would speak for Him. He went on to guide them so they could distinguish a true prophet from **false prophets** who claimed to speak for Him but did not have His authority (Deuteronomy 18:15-20). Jesus knew that false prophets would try to infiltrate the fellowship of His disciples. For that reason, He points out the distinguishing mark of false prophets. They come in **sheep's clothing**. In other words, they appear to be gentle and loving

YOUR NOTES

companions on the journey with Jesus who appear to cultivate a heart of devotion to Him. Their words and actions give the initial impression that God had sent them and that their message can be trusted. In reality, they are **ravenous wolves** who actually have no intention of nurturing believers or giving them guidance that would help them as they walk with Jesus. Instead, they are nothing less than predators who do everything possible to damage believers and seek to obliterate the cause of Christ.

Of course, the pressing question on the minds of growing disciples is how we **recognize** false prophets before they carry out their vicious attacks. Jesus answers that question by teaching us that we will be able to distinguish them by taking a close look at the **fruit** they produce. Although a **thornbush** may produce something that resembles a **grape**, closer inspection will reveal that it's not a real grape. By the same token, something that looks like **figs** may be hanging on the branches of a **thistle**. A careful analysis reveals the truth about the thistle. It will never produce figs.

Jesus uses the image of a tree that was **good** and another tree that was **bad**. From there, He shares the simple and straightforward method for evaluating these teachers. Instead of studying the trunk, examining the limbs, or inspecting the leaves on the tree, taking a long look at the fruit is the best approach. A good tree bears nothing but **good fruit**, and a bad tree only produces **bad fruit**.

With this description, Jesus points His disciples back to the principle He had taught earlier. Their righteousness had to begin inside their hearts. In turn, the words and actions that emanated from their hearts would speak volumes about their intimate relationship with God (Matthew 5:20). He echoes the words of John the Baptist, that bad trees cannot bear good fruit. Consequently, they will be chopped down and set on **fire** because they serve no useful purpose (Matthew 3:8-10).

Next, Jesus focuses on what these false prophets will say in the presence of the Lord. Like believers, false prophets will say that they were devoted to Him, and they will declare Him as Lord. But unlike true believers, their declarations will not represent what's actually in their hearts. Even though they claim devotion to Him, what they say doesn't come from their hearts.

If we're authentic followers of Jesus, we sincerely affirm Him as Lord from our hearts because we have been born again. Our hearts have been transformed because of the gift of salvation He has provided by His grace. Now we belong to Him wholeheartedly and without reservation, and we bow before Him with joyful humility as our King.

False prophets and their companions may say they belong to Jesus, however, mere words will not grant anyone entrance into the **kingdom of heaven**. In fact, words should be viewed with suspicion if what they say is not validated by clear willingness to obey Him. Authentic disciples want to obey God by doing **His will**. Doing His will means living out what Jesus taught about growing as a faithful disciple. Spiritual growth involves looking into our hearts and trusting Him to change us from the inside out. When our hearts are turned toward Him, we submit to Him in obedience. In turn, our words and actions become reflectors of the change that's taken place in the deepest place in our hearts. We obey Him because we know Him intimately and love Him wholeheartedly. In loving obedience to Him, we strive to do what He wants us to every day.

Jesus makes it clear that some who declare Him as Lord may not actually know Him personally at all. Granted, they may know *about* Him. In fact, they may know quite a bit

YOUR NOTES

about Him as they have observed His character in the lives of His devoted followers. They may be very familiar with His life and ministry, and they may have a detailed awareness of His crucifixion and resurrection. In addition, they may have become acquainted with the gospel message that centers on Him, but they never received His gift of salvation. Even though they have heard the good news, they have not truly repented and placed their faith in Him. Accordingly, they have not surrendered themselves to Him in obedience. With the fruit previously described by Jesus, these claims are found to be hollow.

People who say that Jesus is Lord without surrendering to Him in obedience will be held accountable for the reality of their lives. **The day** will come when they face Him in judgment. Later in His ministry, He elaborated on what would happen on the day of judgment as He continued to teach His disciples (Matthew 24:29-51). The day will come when the false followers will be judged by Him. In response, these false followers will claim allegiance to Him. They will support their declaration with testimonies of their works done for Him. They will tell Him about the times they accomplished remarkable spiritual feats **in His name**. These feats include prophesying, driving out **demons**, and performing **miracles**. With testimonies of their extraordinary work on His behalf, they will try to make a convincing argument of their loyalty to Him. Surely these works will give proof of what they have done and He will judge them favorably.

Still, Jesus says that He will **announce** their judgment. Jesus assures us that He's the Good Shepherd who knows His sheep, and His sheep know Him (John 10:14). When Jesus tells the false followers that He **never knew** them, He will underscore the reality that they had never given their lives to Him. Otherwise, He would have known them. Then He will send them out of His presence after judging them as **lawbreakers**. They, like all people, will have had the opportunity to turn to Him for forgiveness and experience the joy of eternal salvation in Him. Instead, they rejected Him and will be accountable for their sin.

Two Foundations (7:24-27)

Following the sobering portrayal of judgment for false followers, Jesus moves on to offer an assurance as well as a warning to His disciples. As they chose to follow Him, they could rest assured that they would not be disappointed with their choice.

He brings up a parable for His disciples, and it starts with the frequently used transition word **therefore**. This signified that the parable had its roots in everything He had taught them on the mountain. They would be wise to take the instruction they had heard seriously and put it into practice. In other words, they needed to **act** on it.

Jesus introduces the parable by describing a person who takes His instruction seriously as a person who constructs a **house on the rock**. Those listening recognized building a house on a foundation of solid rock was important. However, it would have been difficult. Building on a rock meant carving out a flat place large enough to provide enough space for the foundation of the **house**. Carving out such a critical spot would require digging through an unforgiving terrain like a mountainside. It would take a long time and an exhausting amount of hard work. Once the rock slab had been carved, the house could be constructed. Eventually, the house would be completed, and the builder could be pleased with the

YOUR NOTES

finished product. He could rest in the assurance that he had provided a sturdy house for himself and his family.

The sturdiness of the house would be tested when the storm came. Jesus describes a future day where a heavy storm comes with torrential **rain**. The heavy rainfall would make the water levels in the **rivers** rise to a dangerous level. To make matters worse, the gusting **winds** would blow without stopping. The constant, powerful gusts of wind that howled would crash against the **house** on the rock. The pounding would be relentless until the storm finally passed. After the storm, the builder could step outside and inspect the house. He would be pleased and relieved as he observed that his house did not **collapse**. In that moment, he reaps the fruit of the wisdom of building his house **on the rock**.

After comparing His disciples who put His instruction into practice to a house built on a rock, Jesus moves on with another comparison. He compares a person who refuses to take His instruction seriously with a builder who chose to construct his home **on the sand**. For the disciples who listened to Jesus, building a house on the sand meant constructing it near water. They could imagine a builder who decided to build his house on a riverbank. Of course, putting a house next to a river would have plenty of advantages. One advantage in particular had to do with the water itself. The builder of the house on the rock might have to be concerned with getting a regular supply of fresh water to the house. He might need to carry the water from a well or a stream. Whereas, the builder of the house on the sandy riverbank would always have a supply of fresh water close at hand. Another advantage had to do with the convenience of the sand serving as the foundation for the riverside house. The moldable nature of sand meant the builder would not need to invest much energy in transforming the sandy ground into a workable foundation. Getting building supplies to the site would present yet another advantage to the builder of the riverside house. They could be brought by way of the river, which would have been much easier than carrying them by hand to the site of the house built on the rock.

With those and perhaps other advantages in view, the builder of the house on the sand appeared to be making a good decision. Within a little while, his house would be ready to occupy, with possibly less trouble than the builder of the house on the rock.

Just like with the house built on the rock, a fierce storm would eventually come and test the durability of the house built on the sand. The clouds would release relentless torrents of **rain**. Equally disturbing, the water in the river next to the house would rise but never crest. Eventually the swollen river would flood the entire region. Storm **winds** would pound relentlessly against the house. Each new gust of wind would be stronger than the last. Obviously, the riverside house would fail the durability test. To the disappointment and possibly destruction of the builder, it would collapse with a tremendous **crash**.

With the parable, Jesus highlights the consequences of our choices regarding the foundation of our lives. Either our choice will leave us with assurance, or it will warn us of certain disaster. Granted, building our lives on the rock means remaining steadfast in our devotion to Him. We determine that we'll put what He's teaching us into practice without fail. Living this way proves He matters most of all to us, even if taking Him seriously puts us in difficult conditions. By comparison, those who reject the truth of Jesus will lean toward convenience and comfort as the ultimate goal. They might put His instruction to work in their lives, but only if it doesn't inconvenience them.

YOUR NOTES

On the surface, the difference between these two foundations may not be immediately clear. But then the storm will come. It may take the shape of a literal storm, or it may be something worse. It may come in the form of a horrifying medical test result or a report of financial ruin. It may take the shape of a notice from our employer who breaks the bad news that our employment has been terminated. In life, storms of different kinds may come all at once. One storm that is certain to come is that of God's judgment at the end of our lives. If we have not built our lives on the foundation of Christ as our rock, we have no hope to withstand God's judgment and will face ultimate devastation.

Storm damage shows us that we're wise when we build our lives on the rock. Therefore, the teaching of Jesus serves as bedrock for growing disciples. Even more to the point, Jesus Himself is our Rock. When we make Him the foundation of our lives, we can be certain that we've made the wisest decision. Because Jesus remains our priority, we'll be able to endure the storms that come our way, no matter which form they take or how long they last.

Responses (7:28–8:1)

After Jesus points His disciples to the importance of building their lives on a growing relationship with Him, He **finishes** His instruction on the mountain. His disciples had listened in astonishment as He taught. Their amazement came from their awareness of His distinctive **authority**. They sensed that what He said came directly from their Father in heaven. Therefore, they heard His instruction as firsthand discourse. They had not been accustomed to it. **Their scribes** taught in a way that was more like secondhand information. They relied on the insights from previous rabbis before them that had been handed down through the generations of Jewish people. In stark contrast, the instruction of Jesus resonated with them as the direct and living words of God Himself.

Of course, Jesus would provide them with other opportunities to learn about growing as His disciples. The instruction they received on the mountain would serve them well as many began to follow after Him. Having listened to what He had said, they would be able to watch Him as He lived out the truths He proclaimed. Through precept and example, He would reinforce His instruction on the mountain throughout His life and ministry. On the other side of the cross and empty tomb, many would take hold of His instruction even more precisely. They would understand His teaching in keeping with His messianic mission. And they would keep on following Him into their world.

If we are wise, we will join them in following Jesus as His disciples in our world.

YOUR NOTES

YOUR NOTES

PREACHING GUIDE

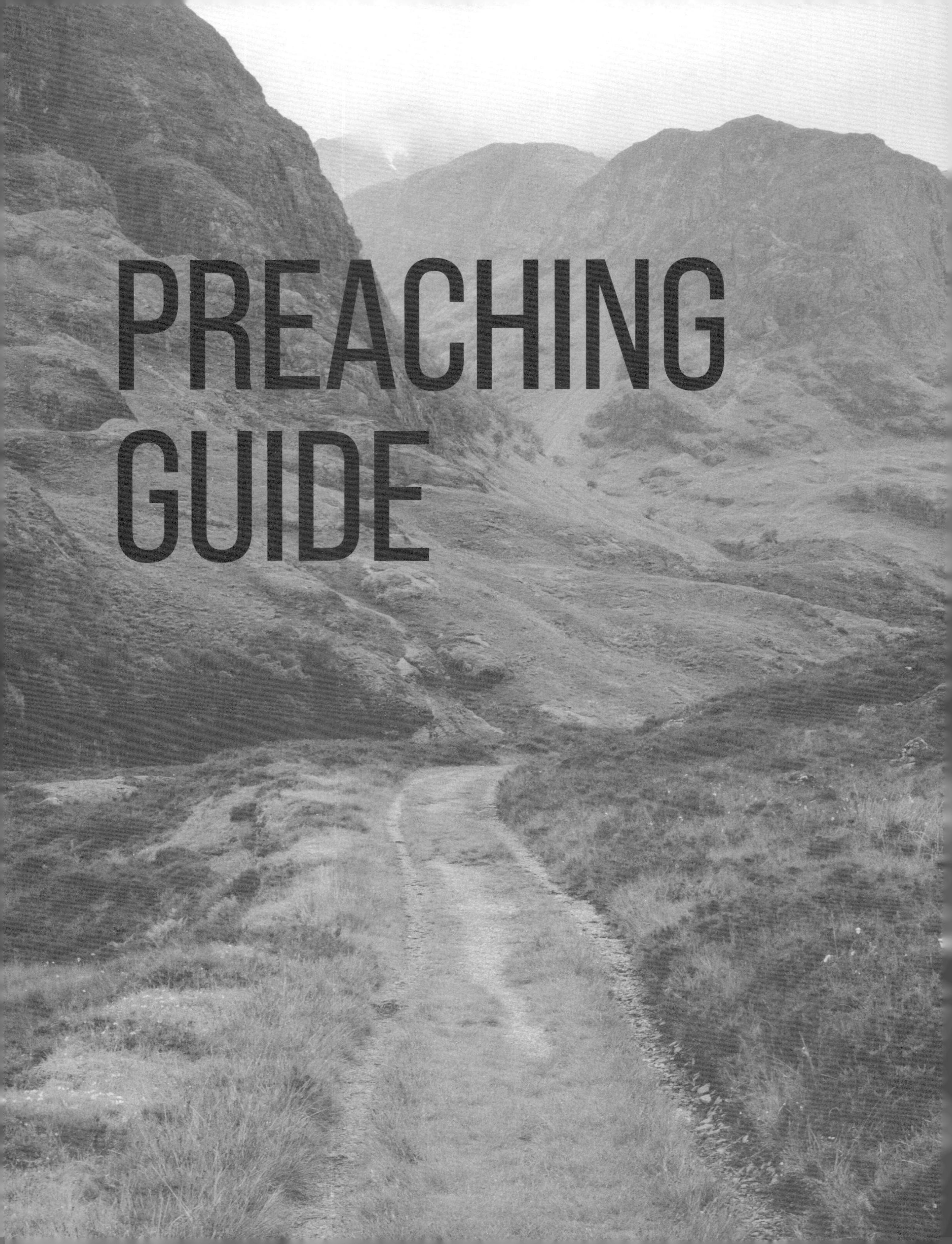

YOUR NOTES

The Sermon on the Mount contains many of Jesus's most memorable sayings such as "blessed are the poor in spirit," "turn the other cheek," "don't judge lest you be judged," and "do to others as you would have them do to you." As a result, Matthew 5–7 has been one of the most studied, written about, and preached upon portion of the Bible throughout the church's history.

CHAPTER 1:
Jesus's (Shocking) Vision for the Truly Blessed Life

Sermon Title: The Secret to True Happiness
Text: Matthew 5:1-16
Focus: Jesus opens His most famous sermon with nine declarations about where to find true happiness. We'll see that how He defines happiness is not what we expect. But like all philosophers and theologians, He's addressing the same question—*How do we find true happiness?*

Introduction:
What do all people at all times want? Is there anything that we can identify as universal and timeless that drives how all humans live? If so, what is it? Those questions are not new. They've been asked and answered for as long as people have been wrestling with what it means to be human. In the Greco-Roman world, before and during the time of Jesus, this question was discussed often by the great philosophers.

The answer they gave was consistent. Likewise, in the first eighteen hundred years of the church this question was asked by theologians and, maybe shockingly to us, they gave the same answer. All people want to be happy.

I. Jesus the Sage (5:1-2)
II. The Happy Life in Relationship to God (5:3-6)
III. The Happy Life in Relationship to Others (5:7-12)
IV. Life as Jesus's Priests in the World (5:13-16)

YOUR NOTES

CHAPTER 2: The Greater Righteousness of the Kingdom

Sermon Title: How to Live Righteously
Text: Matthew 5:17-48
Focus: The Sermon is a carefully crafted literary whole and 5:17-20 are not separate from the verses around them. 5:17-20 provides the thesis statement or guiding argument for the whole central section of the Sermon (5:17–7:12). In this portion of the study we will be looking at 5:17-48, which includes Jesus's big idea in 5:17-20 and the first set of six teachings to explain and apply this to our daily lives (5:21-48). Overall, in 5:17-48 Jesus is teaching us (1) how His entering into the world both confirms and transforms God's instructions to Israel; and (2) how to live righteously, that is, pleasing to God.

Introduction:
What teachings from the Old Testament apply to Christians today? The Hebrew Scriptures are full of instructions from God to His people and Jesus is clearly presented as the Jewish Messiah. It seems reasonable to argue that because God has not changed, these teachings from the Old Testament still apply to followers of Jesus. So are Christians forbidden to get tattoos (Leviticus 19:28) and eat pork (Deuteronomy 14:8)? Are we required to circumcise boys on the eighth day (Genesis 17:9-14) and avoid working on the Sabbath/Saturday so that we can worship God (Exodus 20:8-11)?

Building upon His introduction, Jesus presses into the main topic of His message—what it means to be righteous, that is, what it means to live according to what God says is right. The connection is clear—God cares about our flourishing and this can only be found when we live according to God's ways.

I. Not Abolish but Fulfill (5:17-20)
II. Murder and Anger (5:21-26)
III. Adultery and Lust (5:27-30)
IV. Adultery and Divorce (5:31-32)
V. Oaths and Words (5:33-37)
VI. Retaliation and Vengeance (5:38-42)
VII. Enemies and Love (5:43-48)
VIII. Summing It Up (5:17-20)

CHAPTER 3: Our Praise Problem

YOUR NOTES

Sermon Title: Living as Whole People
Text: Matthew 6:1-21
Focus: Here in 6:1-21 Jesus addresses the disordered desire for the praise that comes from other people, applying it particularly to our religious lives. As with the rest of the Sermon, the point is the same—God wants us to be whole people, people whose outward lives match our inward lives, even as God himself is whole and consistent (5:48).

Introduction:
We humans have a praise problem. Our praise problem works in two directions, the vertical and the horizontal. Our vertical praise problem is that we often love and worship created things rather than the Creator (Romans 1:21-23). This dishonors our God and distorts our souls. The great theologian Augustine helpfully describes sin as our "disordered loves"[1]—we love and worship in a disordered way, loving the wrong things or loving good things but in the wrong degree and order.

But we also have a horizontal praise problem—we all long for the praise and recognition of others. The issue here is complicated. On the one hand, there is nothing wrong with this in that we are designed as communal creatures who need each other's love, affirmation, and encouragement. Any human who never receives this kind of good "praise" will not thrive physically, emotionally, or relationally. Additionally, God has made the world in such a way that we cannot help but praise and honor good and beautiful things in our fellow humans—a beautifully played violin sonata, a perfect goal in the corner of the net in a soccer game, an act of heroism or kindness. These things and these people rightly deserve honor, praise, and accolades.

But on the other hand, just like all our other loves, this good need for praise can get distorted. Our desire for the praise that comes from others can become disordered and we can become dependent on and crave this kind of attention, like an addict.

I. The Opening Exhortation (6:1)
II. The First Examples: Almsgiving (6:2-4)
III. The Second Example: Prayer (6:5-8)
IV. The Lord's Prayer (6:9-15)
V. The Third Example: Fasting (6:16-18)
VI. The Concluding Exhortation (6:19-21)

1. Augustine, *The City of God*, trans. Marcus Dods, with introduction by Thomas Merton (New York: Modern Library, 1950).

YOUR NOTES

CHAPTER 4: The Bridge to Wholeness

Sermon Title: Whole Living with Our Treasure
Text: Matthew 6:19-34
Focus: Disciples of Jesus must once again pursue wholeness. As with responding to God's instructions (5:21-48) and in the practice of our spirituality (6:1-21), true life in God's kingdom will only be found in the way of "greater righteousness." This greater righteousness is not merely external but pays attention to our hearts, our inner person. Whatever we give our heart to is what we give our allegiance to, and therefore, our future (6:21). There are few things in life that have more power to capture our allegiance than money and possessions. Thus, in this next section of applying the principle of 5:20, Jesus turns to the goods of the world and the unhappy result of what happens when we live bifurcated rather than wholehearted lives.

Introduction:
In the ancient world, many people described our ability to see as a function of light emitting from our eyes, like a modern-day flashlight. Thus, the eye is the lamp of the body in the sense that it shines forth what is inside our souls, our hearts, and our inner person. When our eye is "healthy" then this reveals whether our hearts are light/good or dark/evil. The key to understanding what Jesus is saying is paying attention to this Greek word, *haplous*. While "healthy" is not a bad translation, the more fundamental sense of this word is "singular" or "whole" (which is contrasted with "doubleness," as in James 1:8). If our eye is "whole" then this results in and shows that our inner person is light. Thus, we see again the repeated theme in the Sermon of the necessity of our wholeness, consistency, or integrity between the parts of who we are, both inside and out.

I. God and Money (6:22-24)
II. God, Money, and Anxiety (6:25-34)

CHAPTER 5:
The Right Way to Judge

YOUR NOTES

Sermon Title: Whole Living with Other People
Text: Matthew 7:1-12
Focus: Matthew 7:1-12 is the conclusion to the third application of Jesus's exhortation toward greater righteousness. The first application concerned relationships with each other as instructed by Torah (5:21-48). The second application focused on our acts of piety toward God (6:1-21). The third application of greater righteousness applies to our relationship to the goods and people of the world around us (6:19–7:12). In the preceding study (6:19-34) we saw how Jesus exhorts us to be wise in how we think about our relationship to money and possessions. Now Jesus invites us to the same kind of whole-person wisdom when we think about our relationships with other people (7:1-6). Jesus concludes this section by reminding us again of our heavenly Father's care and provision for us (7:7-11), even as he did in 6:25-34.

Introduction:
"Don't judge me!" has become a mantra for many people in our society. It is most often used when someone is aware that what they are doing is morally questionable, spoken with an air of defensiveness. Because Christian morals have been so pervasive in Western civilization and especially in America, many people who utter this phrase are reacting to real or perceived disagreements between their behavior and the teachings of Christianity.

Things get especially sticky when someone who says "Don't judge me" is aware of Jesus's teaching in the Sermon on the Mount. They may not actually know much about the Sermon but Matthew 7:1 is one of those sayings that has woven its way into people's general knowledge. Thus, when someone senses that a Christian is disagreeing with their behavior, the response is often that this "judging" Christian is hypocritical and not following Jesus Himself. "Didn't Jesus Himself say, 'Don't judge'?" is often the vehement response. "How dare you question my choices and my morality while claiming to be a Christian?" Today we will consider Jesus's words on this topic. What does it mean to "judge"? What is a hypocrite and how do we avoid being one?

I. Evaluating Rightly (7:1-2)
II. Evaluating People Rightly (7:3-6)
III. Evaluating God Rightly (7:7-11)
IV. Living Wisely (7:12)

YOUR NOTES

CHAPTER 6:
Two Ways of Living

Sermon Title: The Right Foundation
Text: Matthew 7:13–8:1
Focus: The conclusion to the Sermon consists of three subsections of teaching—7:13-14, 7:15-23, and 7:24-27. Each of these teachings use metaphors or parabolic images to invite us to feel the weight of Jesus's words. The broad and narrow paths, the true and false prophets, and the wise and foolish builders make clear that our response to Jesus cannot be neutral—it is a choice of one path or the other. Throughout this conclusion the same Sermonwide theme of wholeness can be found.

Introduction:
When the foundation of a house is weakened, damage and destruction follow. It is with this kind of vivid and memorable image (including this particular metaphor) that Jesus concludes His masterful message, the Sermon on the Mount.

The third and final image in Jesus's Sermon is appropriately climactic. Jesus describes two different people who build their houses in two different ways. One lays the foundation of his house on sand and the other on rock. The difference between these two people and their respective houses is described as wise versus foolish because sooner or later each house will undergo trial and stress. When it does, the wisdom or foolishness of the foundation work will be revealed. The rock-built house will be able to withstand the winds and water while the sandy foundation will give way, resulting in destruction of the whole house in dramatic fashion.

I. The Broad and Narrow Paths (7:13-14)
II. True and False Prophets (7:15-23)
III. The Wise and Foolish Builders (7:24-27)
IV. The Response of the Crowd (7:28–8:1)